G000141682

Real Life Diaries

LIVING WITH
ENDOMETRIOSIS

Inspiring true stories about finding hope
and managing life with endometriosis

LYNDA CHELDELIN FELL

with

CHRISTA HALL

CARMELA POLLOCK

FOREWORD BY

CARMELA POLLOCK

A portion of proceeds from the sale of this book is
donated to Endometriosis Research Center, a
nonprofit organization. For more information, visit
www.endocenter.org.

Real Life Diaries
Living with Endometriosis – 1st ed.
Inspiring true stories about finding hope and managing life with
endometriosis
Lynda Cheldelin Fell/Christa Hall/Carmela Pollock
Real Life Diaries www.GriefDiaries.com

Cover Design by AlyBlue Media, LLC
Interior Design by AlyBlue Media LLC
Published by AlyBlue Media, LLC

ISBN: 978-1-944328-52-8
Library of Congress Control Number: 2016918773
AlyBlue Media, LLC
Ferndale, WA 98248
www.AlyBlueMedia.com

PRINTED IN THE UNITED STATES OF AMERICA

Living with Endometriosis

DEDICATION

This book is dedicated to women around
the world who live with endometriosis.

Living with Endometriosis

CONTENTS

BY CARMELA POLLOCK

FOREWORD

Living with endometriosis, a painful and indiscriminate disease, is much more complex than putting up with just misplaced tissue. Although it affects millions of women around the world, it remains misunderstood and largely unknown because it's an invisible disorder. Some people understand, but many do not. With one in ten women worldwide suffering (not including those yet to be diagnosed), and a diagnosis timeline of up to ten years, our hope is that the Real Life Diaries series can help empower women to share their journey and receive the support they need.

My journey with endometriosis taught me the extent of my resilience, and gave me courage to push through those debilitating moments. It tested my resolve with the long and difficult journey toward diagnosis and the daily effects of living with chronic illness that included managing pain and associated fatigue.

It was 1995. I was twenty-five years old and had already spent years fielding people's well-meaning comments, misdiagnosis and chronic pain. Tired of having to explain myself, I resorted to putting on a brave face thinking it was just easier to do. I was alone and woke to debilitating pain that left me unable to walk. The bed sheets covered in blood, I was fatigued and consumed with pain that engulfed my body. I called the ambulance service and was rushed to the hospital, where I was tended to immediately. I was hemorrhaging, in agony, scared, and confused. Days later, I was officially given a diagnosis: endometriosis.

And so the road to understanding began. This diagnosis brought great relief—I wasn't a hypochondriac, as stated by a doctor. However, this period in my life also brought sorrow when I received news from my gynecologist that due to the condition of my uterus and ovaries, conceiving and carrying a child to term would be near impossible. I felt grief for the first time—an ambiguous loss. My life was turned upside down, but I refused to accept the possibility of being childless and made sure it didn't undermine my relationship with my husband.

Despite overwhelming odds, my miracle child was born in 2006. He represented, then and now, that I am indeed the creator of my story. He is a tangible expression of the growth and tenacity of my spirit, regardless of the diagnosis. He is my personal joy and treasure.

Helen Keller once said, "Walking with a friend in the dark is better than walking alone in the light." If you live with endometriosis, the following stories have been written by courageous women who have been in your shoes and walked the same path. Perhaps the shoes are a different size or style, but may you find comfort in these stories and the understanding that you aren't truly alone on the journey. For we walk ahead, behind, and right beside you.

CARMELA POLLOCK
www.soulworksessential.com

BY LYNDA CHELDELIN FELL

PREFACE

One night in 2007, I had a vivid dream. I was the front passenger in a car and my daughter Aly was sitting behind the driver. Suddenly the car missed a curve in the road and sailed into a lake. The driver and I escaped the sinking car, but Aly did not. My beloved daughter was gone. The only evidence left behind was a book floating in the water where she disappeared.

Two years later, on August 5, 2009, that horrible nightmare became reality when Aly died as a backseat passenger in a car accident. Returning home from a swim meet, the car carrying Aly and two teammates was T-boned by a father coming home from work. My beautiful daughter took the brunt of the impact and died instantly. She was fifteen years old.

Just when I thought life couldn't get any worse, it did. My hubby buried his grief in the sand. He escaped into eighty-hour workweeks, more wine, more food, and less talking. His blood pressure shot up, his cholesterol went off the chart, and the perfect storm arrived on June 4, 2012. Without warning, he suddenly began drooling and couldn't speak. My 46-year-old soulmate was having a major stroke.

Jamie survived the stroke but couldn't speak, read, or write, and his right side was paralyzed. Still reeling from the loss of our daughter, I again found myself thrust into a fog of grief so thick, I couldn't see through the storm. Adrenaline and autopilot resumed their familiar place at the helm.

In the aftermath of losing Aly and my husband's subsequent stroke, I eventually discovered that swapping stories helps us feel less alone—and offers others an opportunity to better understand. As the Swedish proverb goes, "Shared sorrow is half a sorrow." *Real Life Diaries* was born and built on that belief.

Sharing stories about endometriosis allows us to fully examine the profound impact such a disease has on the lives of women of all ages, and in doing so perhaps a little bit of healing takes place for both readers and writers. Each woman who bravely penned her story in this book shared the deepest, most intimate parts of her life in hopes that those who walk this journey needn't feel alone any longer. It is there in the heartfelt words and poignant stories where those who share the path find comfort, understanding, and hope.

Wishing you healing and hope for the rest of your journey.

Warm regards,

Lynda Cheldelin Fell

CREATOR, REAL LIFE DIARIES
www.LyndaFell.com

CHAPTER ONE

The Beginning

It's hard to explain to someone who has no idea what it's like to feel pain and sickness on the inside while looking fine on the outside. -ENDOBODY

Endometriosis is an indiscriminate disorder affecting millions of women and girls, yet no two journeys are the same. Some live in pain for years before a diagnosis is finally rendered. Others find speedy support and treatment early on. To fully appreciate the unique stories, it is helpful to understand the different journeys. In this chapter each writer shares the beginning of her story.

*

ADRIEANNE BEASLEY
Adrieanne was diagnosed with
endometriosis in 2014 at age 31

I first began having symptoms of endometriosis when I was thirteen years old. I had extremely heavy periods accompanied by severe pain, and sometimes missed school as a result.

At age sixteen, my family doctor put me on birth control to help control my cycles and lessen the bleeding, as I was becoming anemic. This helped a little bit but I still had pain and spotting between periods. My doctor said this was genetic, as my mom had similar problems. Over the years, I saw many different gynecologists and doctors who all brushed my symptoms off as normal, or that "it was all in my head." I was prescribed antidepressants to help with the anxiety and depression that I was experiencing.

In 2008, I tried for two years to get pregnant with my then-husband and was unsuccessful, even after hormone treatments. This was a very difficult time and my husband began to treat me extremely poorly and became very emotionally abusive. He also started having multiple affairs. I felt so ashamed that I was unable to get pregnant and that he was now cheating on me! Not once was endometriosis mentioned as a possible disease that I might have.

I thought that losing weight would help with the pain and heavy periods, as I had been overweight my entire life. I lost over sixty pounds but it didn't help. In 2012, a friend was diagnosed with endometriosis and then it crossed my mind that it was something I too might have. However, none of my doctors at the time believed me.

In early 2012, I got divorced and then developed an addiction to cocaine, due in part to the pain and exhaustion I felt, both physically and mentally. My periods were quite irregular and heavy at this point, and I couldn't handle it anymore. An IUD was placed in February which helped to control my cycles a bit, finally giving some relief.

In January 2013, I moved with my new boyfriend to Edmonton, Alberta. I got clean and started to refocus on my health. It was then when my endometrial symptoms worsened, and I started missing work due to pain.

In April 2013, I was referred to a gynecologist who actually believed that there was something wrong with me. I had all the standard symptoms of endometriosis such as heavy bleeding, painful periods, pain during sex, spotting, abdominal and back cramping, painful bowel movements, difficulty becoming pregnant, chronic pelvic pain at any time during my cycle, constipation, and diarrhea. During this time I also had an irregular pap smear. After several tests and a colposcopy, it was revealed that I had early stage cervical cancer.

On March 17, 2014, my gynecologist performed a laparoscopy. This was originally supposed to be a diagnostic procedure, however they found that I had stage four endometriosis. The surgery took a total of four and a half hours and they removed many areas of endometriosis from my bowel down to my rectum. It was such a relief finally hearing that I wasn't crazy and that all my symptoms were real. I now had an actual diagnosis!

On April 2, 2014, I had surgery to remove part of my cervix, which was successful. But a few months later my symptoms returned, and they were worse than before. I was very disappointed, as my gynecologist told me that surgery is usually successful in reducing symptoms for up to five years. I am currently struggling with trying to get in with a certified excision specialist, however there are a lot of politics involved with gynecologists in Canada. I am hoping that one day I can get in to see an excision specialist who can perform my surgery successfully, and then I can finally be pain-free.

In August 2014, I married the love of my life. He has been my rock and a great supporter. I am so lucky to have someone like this in my life as I know many women who don't, and going through this alone can be extremely difficult. A solid support system is so important. My husband, friends, and family have all been really understanding with everything I've gone through.

For a few months, I had experienced extreme pelvic pain and bleeding. After having a hysterosonogram it was revealed that I had two uterine fibroids. On July 7, 2016, I had a hysteroscopy and myomectomy to remove the fibroids. Unfortunately they have come back, which is common.

As far as pain management goes, I've tried numerous things. I do my best to be active every day in one form or another, whether it be yoga, weightlifting or cardio. Some days the pain is very bad and I cannot go to the gym. It is also important to realize when I should rest and take it easy. It's all about balance. I've tried acupuncture for pain which I find helpful.

In April 2016, I decided to completely change my diet to an anti-inflammatory one. I have eliminated all meat, dairy, gluten, processed foods, sugar, alcohol and caffeine from my diet. I've noticed that I have less abdominal bloating and cramping. I do plan to try other forms of pain management in the future, such as pelvic floor physiotherapy.

My struggle to get proper care for my endometriosis continues. I feel that it's important to be an advocate for your own health. Over the past few years, I have had to push for proper care for myself as no one else was going to do it for me, which was unfortunate.

In March 2016, I came across a local endometriosis support group. I have since joined several groups, all of which have given me more information about endometriosis than I could've ever imagined. I will forever be grateful to these women for helping me through this painful journey. Sometimes my fight can be extremely hard, and there are days when I don't think that I can do it. All I can do is hope that one day we can find a cure for endometriosis so we can end the pain that so many women have to go through.

*

SHILOH BRITT
Shiloh was diagnosed with
endometriosis in 2011 at age 22

At twenty-seven, I never thought I would have to say goodbye to any part of me. An appendix sure, who uses those anyway? Maybe a kidney in a pinch, something I didn't really need. At twenty-seven, I wasn't thinking about kids. It wasn't that I was thinking of not having them, kids just weren't on my mind at all. Maybe in the future, but definitely not now.

It's hard to explain the emotion of having something taken away that I didn't know I wanted. Something I never gave much thought to, aside from those five to seven days each month when I cursed its existence, but integrally knew I always needed. To have something that was quite literally a part of me taken away was confusing, even more so because it was by my own direct choosing. The choice was mine. I did this to myself—and will always hold that weight.

At twenty-seven, I was old—a shell of who I once was. I looked around at my peers and was envious of what they could do, how they could push their bodies without seemingly any repercussions. I envied how they could work out at the gym and play frisbee at Boulevard Park, fall down and brush it off, swim and dive and feel free, and do all those things I, too, once took for granted.

At twenty-seven, my body was withered with pain. It was tired from fighting an invisible fight, of pushing on when every nerve screamed in defeat. Each movement was costly, and a day didn't go by when I didn't rely on a cornucopia of meds to manage the pain. But it wasn't being managed—some days I was unable to get out of bed, and the harsh pain medications dampened my once vibrant demeanor.

At twenty-seven, I was a bitch. My temper was short and my patience shorter. I had no time for more drama than I already had in my life. My coworkers thought me cold and demanding, and even my customers thought I was brash or rude. When I finally came to these harsh realizations, I cried—this was not me. The constant pain I was in manifested in ways I never even realized. I was a terrible employee, never dependable because I could never predict the painful flares. I often went home due to the intensity of the pain, and more often than not, would be forced to call out sick. I feared that my disease, and inability to control it, would leave me permanently disabled and unable to work. It's hard to express how much you love your job when no one wants to work with you on account of your unpredictable pain.

At twenty-seven, my life was on hold waiting for a miracle, a miracle I myself didn't believe would ever come. Time is funny that way—after years of constant pain, you forget what it's like to live without it. You wonder how you could ever feel so free... you fear you never will again.

At twenty-seven, I was shunned. Made to feel like some sideshow circus act. Everyone, look at the barren woman! No longer able to have children, I felt like a burden to my family. My mother-in-law, who found many faults in me, added fuel to her fire upon learning she would never have biological grandchildren. She pointed out that I was useless, and encouraged her son to seek a divorce.

At twenty-seven, I was given a rare chance at the possibility of a pain-free life. No guarantee, by any means; but a possibility when all others had been exhausted. The cost: future children. The firstborn girl who was to have my middle name—the name handed to firstborn daughters by their mothers for the past five generations. A son's middle name would be that of my husband's, to carry on a long-lived tradition in his family.

At twenty-seven, I was given a choice: to go on living my shell of a life that held uncertainty of my ability to leave the bed, or undergo surgery and take a chance toward freedom from the daily pain I had known for the past ten years.

At twenty-seven, I had to be selfish and remember that my life was worth living—really living.

On February 5, I underwent a total hysterectomy. Out came my uterus. Out came my cervix. Out came my fallopian tubes. My ovaries remain intact only because I fought to keep them against my doctor's judgment. But my doctor wasn't a woman; he had no way of knowing how removing everything and throwing me into a forced menopause would have been too much...a portion of my bladder was surgically cauterized.

The last thing I remember before the anesthesia took effect was being wheeled into a cold, bright operating room and becoming overwhelmed with emotions. I cried.

I cried because I was scared.

I cried for my mom.

I cried for my husband.

I cried for losing fertility and with it my future children. I cried because of my terrible relationship with my mother-in-law.

I cried for being in so much pain for so long. I cried from exhaustion. I cried in relief.

I cried because I was alone, and I cried because it was the only thing left to do.

It's been months and I'm still crying. In some ways, I think I will always be crying.

It's hard not to be bitter when the first thing you see on Facebook in the morning is a baby announcement, or pictures of beautiful newborns being cuddled by their smiling, albeit, tired parents. This is something I will never personally know, and there's a definite pang of grief over this. My husband and I had always talked of having our own kids, but it was always far in the future. After all, we figured we had plenty of time. Turns out we were wrong.

When Mitch and I were newly engaged (he was twenty-five, I was twenty-three), one doctor advised me to just get pregnant, as this would alleviate my pain, for a time anyway. I remember staring at this young doctor, who was not a specialist in this field. How could he even suggest such a thing? I had recently returned to school and Mitch had recently graduated. We were as stereotypical of broke college students as you could get. What followed was a very raw conversation between my fiancé and me. In the end, we decided my health had to be the priority. We could always adopt or foster and still be great parents. Besides, for now we had our three furry babies.

At twenty-seven, I questioned everything. My faith. My career path. My friendships. My marriage. Especially my marriage.

At twenty-seven, I was a student who was mere quarters away from a degree. As my health failed and the endometriosis took hold, my good grades started to slip. As my As became Bs, and Bs dropped to Cs, I took an incomplete in one class. I had to take a quarter off when I had surgery, then struggled when I returned with a stupidly heavy course load the next quarter. I assumed that having the surgery would somehow fix things, that that would be the end of it after a bit of R and R. I couldn't have been more wrong. At twenty-seven, I learned that surgery is only a step in the healing process. The harsh reality is that surgery opens the door to more pain, and more healing.

At twenty-seven, my doctor didn't tell me what to expect beyond the physical. He didn't recommend that I seek emotional support outside my family, and he didn't relay how hard it would be for them to understand. Truth be told, at twenty-seven I was so caught up in trying to be strong, I may not have listened if he had.

At twenty-seven, I learned the value of communication...that there are some sensations, thoughts, and emotions that cannot be conveyed no matter the syntax and jargon juxtaposed.

At twenty-seven, I became so lost in my own despair that I had to write my way out. In the weeks before surgery, I wrote my best friend who lived across the country every day. Pen to paper, and paper to envelope. I wrote of my pain, fears, hopes and dreams, and how much I wished my dearest friend was there to tell me it would all be okay. Today, I'm still writing, and she's still listening.

At twenty-seven, I became a statistic.

At twenty-seven, I outwardly looked pregnant. My belly was swollen like that of a third trimester mother-to-be. My back was sore and my steps calculated. I felt daily nausea and spent more time in the bathroom than I would like to admit. But there was no glow. No life within my own. There was just endometriosis. And it consumed me.

At twenty-seven, I was my disease. I had withered to become all it was. I was my swollen belly, my grayish skin, my bloodshot eyes. This all-encompassing disease had taken over my life and stolen my identity. I had solemnly accepted this. I was endometriosis and I feared that is all I would ever be.

My best friend, blissfully unaware of the depth of my ordeal, would often text me surmising when she might become an auntie. I began to feel the societal pressure that comes after we marry, the pressure to have kids. It's everywhere. Calling to make a gynecological appointment, the receptionist's first question is "How far along are you?" Fighting back tears, I had to say "I'm not," and knowing that I would never be. My doctor's office brims with darling photos of newborn announcements, every room overflows with picture-perfect adoration of little ones new to the world. I began to hate going to my doctor and sometimes ignored minor issues because of these photos, resulting in those issues escalating.

In going through all this, I've learned that I cannot avoid what makes me uncomfortable. It helps no one, especially not myself. Society, on the other hand, has much to learn. And that's the problem: society doesn't talk about women's reproductive health. It's taken for granted. In this society it is taboo to talk about a hysterectomy, it's one of those words that's spoken in hushed tones while looking over one's shoulder for possible eavesdroppers. You will never see the topic of hysterectomy on one of the glamorous magazines in the newsstand, nor will you hear it highlighted in the nightly news. Medical clinics have the pamphlets discretely tucked away, and schools dare not teach of such a thing in their sex education classes.

Mitch has known me only as sickly; he has only known me with limitations. He never knew me before the endometriosis took hold. He never knew the girl who took off for long random runs without a destination in mind though usually ending at the beach where small shore treasures would be stuffed into the sports bra for the jog home. He didn't know the adventurer who climbed sheer rock faces and then dove into the frigid sea below. He didn't know the scuba diver who loved diving the San Juan Islands to spy on octopi or spook swimming crabs. He had yet to meet the practical joker who loved nothing more than a good laugh—usually at her own expense. Nor did he know the water bug who was eager to experience anything that might bring her closer to the water. He hadn't met the environmental activist, or the Special Olympics softball coach. He had never seen the energetic, goofy and clumsy extrovert.

He knew only what my pain allowed me to be: a quiet introvert, a sullen, lost soul who was consumed by the disease.

It's been a few months since surgery, and life has greatly changed. I try to be optimistic, but every time I feel abdominal pain I worry the endometriosis has returned, that surgery didn't work and I had a hysterectomy for nothing. I know that statistically the likelihood of the disease returning is slim, but the fear remains. My husband reminds me to look to logic rather than emotions. He has learned the hard way to never tell me to stop being so emotional. Logically, I know

the healing process is slow, and that laying low and allowing my bo
to heal are challenging for me.

At twenty-seven, I realized that I could turn my ordeal into
something positive.

At twenty-seven, I lie awake and cry at night. Sometimes all night
long. My husband snores loudly next to me, blissfully unaware of the
hell I struggle with while lying beside him. I wordlessly curse at him
for not knowing my ordeal, for not understanding it. I go on facing
my own inner hell, wondering if I'll ever see light. I know it will pass.
It always does. But the fact remains that I feel as though I am a different
person since waking up from a hysterectomy. Suddenly being unable
to bear children had changed me, as I always suspected it would.

At twenty-seven, I wasn't prepared to face an emotional rollercoaster. I wasn't prepared for how the relationship with my husband
would change. How can you tell the man you married that suddenly
you're not so sure any more? How can you tell him that he needs to
move on in life, and leave you? That you fear things won't change in
time to save your own marriage? How can you tell him to go on and
be a father, have the children he's always wanted, live that life he had
always dreamed of—with someone else? Someone who never had to
say goodbye to her uterus?

Even more months have passed now, and in two months I will be
done with twenty-seven. I will face twenty-eight same as I do every
day, with gratitude that I was able to have this experience. I find that
the saying "You never know how strong you are until being strong is

:e you have," is more accurate now than ever before.

isn't going anywhere. But maybe, just maybe, if we all

we can show that we are not going anywhere either.

*

EMMA CLIFTON
Emma was diagnosed with
endometriosis in 2015 at age 30

At the age of fourteen, I started to experience a relentless stitch-like pain in my side, along with bowel issues, bad period pain and horrible rectal spasms that left me crippled on the bathroom floor. I went to the general practitioner and they sent me for a colonoscopy, as Crohn's disease ran in my family. I was diagnosed with irritable bowel syndrome, IBS, and told to change my diet. I started to make changes in my diet and noticed a small difference, but could still eat all the things I was told to avoid and it wouldn't always affect me.

When I first moved out at age nineteen, I decided I wanted to live in Northern Queensland. I was living with three boys in a bit of a party house, working days at a cafe and working nights doing promotional work for a local nightclub. It's fair to say my poor liver suffered greatly due to alcohol consumption during the six months I lived there.

Some mornings I would get up to go to the toilet and be so scared of having a bowel movement, as the rectal spasms were at their worst during this time. I would be halfway through my movement and have to stop, get off the toilet, and curl up in a ball on the floor of the bathroom for a few very painful minutes before it would subside. I chalked it up to my poor diet and excess alcohol consumption, and blamed it on IBS.

There was a break between the age of twenty-two and twenty-five when my symptoms subsided. I was traveling through Europe for seven months of this, living in London for three months and then returning to Australia and moving in with a friend on the Mornington Peninsula. These were probably the happiest and craziest years of my life. I got to travel with my best friends. When I returned home, I lived and worked with a stranger who soon became one of my closest friends, and still is to this day. It was while living with this friend that I met Rhett, and he swept me off my feet.

Within three months, I moved into Rhett's house and we were living a very happy life. About six to eight months after moving in together, I was very stressed at work. Rhett had returned to playing football which took up a lot of time. He was also the captain, and his drinking and social calendar increased quite a lot. We fought about this and also about my work, as he was tired of hearing me complain about a new issue at work every week. I noticed the pain in my side started to come back, along with painful periods and painful sex.

One day after Rhett left for work, I was midcycle and having serious pain. I stayed in bed all day taking pain killers, but nothing was making the pain subside. Rhett got home from work and sat with me for a while before going to football training. About twenty minutes after he left, I begged him to come back and take me to the emergency room. The pain had risen to a level I had never experienced before.

We were in the car on the way to the hospital and I felt like I was having contractions. I would have an intense wave of heat, pain, shaking, and nausea and needed Rhett to pull over each time so I could vomit from pain. We waited in emergency for six hours. They gave me stronger pain killers that finally dulled the pain, however I was dehydrated and still needed to see a doctor.

Rhett was getting very irritated at this point and wanted to go home, as he believed I was better off at home in my own bed until the morning. I discharged myself, even after the nurses suggesting it was not a good idea, and went home. The following morning I went to the general practitioner and they ran blood tests. My CA 125 level was abnormally high and there was fluid on the pouch of Douglas. They sent me for three different ultrasounds, and one showed a cyst on my right ovary. I was given the option to monitor it and if it got bigger and symptoms persisted, then I could have a laparoscopy.

Rhett and I were in the process of building a new house and were watching every dollar. I didn't have private health insurance and was very nervous about going through the public system to have a laparoscopy, so I put it off. Our relationship started to show the cracks at this point, as it hurt for me to have sex and Rhett had a high sex drive. We still had sex however I didn't always enjoy it, and it would always have to be the same way to minimize pain.

We finally moved into our new house and things started to really decline. I had frequent migraines, anxiety and pain. Rhett spent more and more time at the football club, not coming home until all hours of the morning, and every time with an excuse. He had a separate phone and I discovered he was on dating websites. Each and every time he said it was never him, apparently it was a friend using his identity.

I went home one afternoon after work. Before Rhett arrived home, I packed my things and decided I needed some time away. I left him a note saying I didn't want to speak to him. I said he needed to think about what he wanted and whether that included me. I lasted six very long weeks without contact. After six weeks, we agreed that we didn't want to separate. I moved back in after a lot of promises that things would change. The first weekend back home he was out with the boys at the football club. He called me to say he was going out and broke our dinner plans. I was heartbroken and I knew we were in for a slippery slope to failure.

Things got dramatically worse and Rhett's narcissistic side hit a new level. He stopped wanting to have sex. After investigation, I discovered he was having an affair with one of the netballers at the football club. During this horrible year, I lost ten kilograms and my health was deteriorating rapidly. I looked very sick and was constantly having to take time off work.

I left Rhett, we sold the house, and I would like to say I never looked back, but I hit rock bottom. Luckily I was living with close friends who provided amazing support. I started practicing yoga again, which I hadn't done in years as Rhett thought that "spiritual stuff" was a load of crap. In the yoga studio, I felt a sense of calm wash over me, and stay with me for the remainder of the day and night. I increased my practice and was also having healing sessions. My symptoms were still there, but I was using yoga and meditation in place of excess pain killers and found that this was helping. I felt the best I had felt in as long as I could remember. I decided that if I could recover from this without antidepressants, while also reducing my pain medication, then I wanted others to be able to as well. I decided to do yoga teacher training in Bali. I came back from Bali, completely changed my diet, and became even more passionate about health and well-being.

This was a time for change and new beginnings for me. I decided that enough was enough; I didn't want this ovarian cyst to affect future relationships, and I booked a laparoscopy. I went in for a thirty-minute procedure but came out three hours later on morphine and having to stay overnight. They discovered stage four endometriosis and had to remove it all. They also discovered very early signs on my bowel which explained the years of painful bowel movements.

Since surgery I have again changed my diet, got a new job, and am teaching yoga on weekends. I decided that I didn't want to stop my periods and instead preferred a natural approach to my journey with endometriosis, and here I am nine months later.

*

SHANDI CLOUSE
Shandi was diagnosed with
endometriosis in 2015 at age 27

For me, it wasn't just the pain or nausea that marked when everything changed, it was the lack of knowledge. When symptoms hit one afternoon in September, I swore it was just an ovarian cyst rupturing, a common problem I already had. I curled into a ball in my living room chair in tears, trying not to move for hours. I couldn't eat or sleep, despite my husband Eric's encouragement. There was no end to the sharp, stabbing pains in my abdomen. Wave after wave brought another round of sobbing and wondering what could possibly be wrong with me.

By noon the next day, the gnawing pain still hadn't let up. I was at wits end and still on the precipice of throwing up, so I made a call to see my doctor later that afternoon. Much to my surprise she blamed my irritable bowel syndrome instead, acting as if it couldn't possibly be that bad and deflecting the conversation to other things. I persisted that it had to be a rupture; I had felt this pain before. Finally, after an hour, she caved in and finally referred me to a gynecologist—something I had been requesting for months.

Defeated, I went home and tried to carry on with my normal routine with no luck. I got dizzy every time I stood up, rapidly started losing weight, and the pain seemed to never cease. It took a month for the referral to go through and by this time I had dropped to ninety-two pounds, igniting even more fear about the situation. It was here that finally someone understood.

The gynecologist was well educated in endometriosis, and though he didn't mention it until after my exams and ultrasounds came back, he had suspicions from the first appointment. Even all that took another two months to be finished, and finally my laparoscopic surgery was scheduled for the end of November, which brought about the very words I dreaded to hear: stage two adenomyosis.

I remember calling my best friend Josie from the parking lot and she tried for two hours to calm me down, the diagnosis spinning like a hurricane in my head as I told her my options through tears. I was given a week to decide between Lupron or a partial hysterectomy. I agonized over every detail, every bit of research I could find, before caving in and scheduling the surgery, despite being told that I would be back within a few months to have my ovaries removed as well.

The days leading up to that were a mess. I cried randomly, and often curled up on the bathroom floor with Hades, my service dog. I struggled just to get dressed to take my daughters to school, and once outside the house I tried to put on my best face.

In truth, I was shattered. The dream Eric and I had of having a son was ripped from us, and memories of my angel baby crept in often. I can say there were still good days when I could function, which I made the very best of, but most days I was down and barely holding on through the seemingly never-ending flare ups.

I found solace only within my hula hoop and retreated to our bedroom often, headphones blaring and a plastic circle clutched tightly in my hands. It became my meditation; carefully choosing songs that spoke to me and dancing until I could fake a smile to the world again. In the coming months, hula hooping would continue to grant me that same safe haven during the turmoil.

The day before my hysterectomy was my youngest daughter Luna's fifth birthday, and I was an absolute mess. Despite everything I did to make it a wonderful day for her, and to try to be just a normal family, I still had to step away to hide my tears over the thought that she truly was my last child. She would never know what it was like to be a big sister, as her older sister Trinity did.

On the morning of January 19, Eric drove us to the hospital blaring my favorite music and talking about random things. I responded to texts from a few close friends, feigning as much strength as I could. Upon checking in, I faced a blur of paperwork that painfully cemented my decision. And before I knew it, I was wheeled away.

Waking up turned into one of my worst nightmares. I had a bad reaction to the anesthesia and though I still don't remember exactly what happened, I was informed that I started apologizing to Eric, hysterical about how I couldn't give him a son, and wondering how he could even look at me with what I had done. At one point, I was told, I even passed out from the pain, too incoherent to remotely realize what was going on. The entire experience was hellish, and to this day I still feel guilty for the heartbreak I caused him in my delirious state.

Once home, I started to come back to reality and that's when it really hit the hardest. For two months afterward I clawed up from a very dark depression, probably the worst episode I've had in years. Late one night, my friend Josie mentioned that I should write it all down. That same night I stayed up, a bundle of tears and cigarettes and crunched up paper until it all came out on six pages. Everything I wished I had known, every horrible feeling I had kept locked inside, every shred of strength I had went onto the paper and for the first time in months, I finally felt a bit of peace. With her encouragement, I sent in my writing to Chronic Illness on The Mighty and much to my surprise it was published on the last day of Endometriosis Awareness Month. I was astounded at the amount of love I received afterwards. Within hours, it had been shared over three hundred times and the comments flowed in from women who felt the exact same way I did, thanking me for speaking out. To this date, it is still one of the most healing moments I've had during my journey with endometriosis. To know my pain and struggle has made a difference to others suffering through the same obstacles somehow made it easier to cope.

Unfortunately, my doctor's previous prediction came just two months after surgery. My flares started to increase to a scarily similar level as before and I ended up back in my gynecologist's office, as terrified as I was the first time. My exam led him to believe that my endometriosis was being agitated by what he believed to be interstitial cystitis, and I was referred to a urologist who confirmed it as my fifth chronic illness after a few months.

As of now, I am trying to get it under control before we make the decision about whether to proceed with surgery sooner rather than later for my endometriosis and to remove my ovaries.

The journey has been long and hard, but throughout it I have been truly blessed with not just amazing friends and family, but with opportunities to use my story to help others. Though I still wage war against my body, I've come a long way in learning my limits and how to cope within them using support and the sheer will to keep fighting. I take it one day at a time and take nothing for granted. I know all too well that my health and my life can drastically change in an instant, and I use that as motivation to continue chasing my dreams.

I'm proud of my husband and daughters who fight selflessly alongside me through the rough days, and I am grateful for all this path has taught me. Endometriosis has taken much from me, but for them, myself and for every woman who battles this terrible illness, I carry on. My work with Hoopus: WereWolf HopeCraft has allowed me not only to heal, but to reach out to others who are struggling and return the helping hand I so desperately needed myself at one time.

My friend Josie lost her long time battle to Lupus just three months ago, so we continue her mission in her honor of showing how hula hooping has greatly impacted our lives with endometriosis and other chronic illnesses in a positive way. Her unconditional love showed me that even in the wake of the worst times, I cannot and will not give up. I am one of thousands of endometriosis warriors and only together can we stand tall against this disease.

*

PATRICIA CONNELLY
Patricia was diagnosed with
endometriosis in 2014 at age 33

I've always had really bad period pains and very heavy flows. I was taken to doctor after doctor. I was told there was nothing to worry about or the pain was all in my head. When I was eight, my mother had a total hysterectomy. The doctors said she had sores all over her uterus, but never looked into what those sores were. I went on with my life and dealt with the period pains. I finally had enough and started going to doctors again after the pains started to be constant and I was finally told I had endometriosis. I was sent to yet another doctor who had to look up endometriosis on the internet. I was so disappointed. After taking pills for almost a year, she finally did a hysterectomy. She said I did have endometriosis, and that she got it all out and that I had nothing to worry about. About three months later the pain had returned so I went back to the endometriosis doctor. She told me I no longer had endometriosis because she got it all. I took papers with me that I printed off the internet, saying endometriosis does come back. She told me to go back to my regular doctor and have a MRI, so I did. The MRI showed that I have a thick wall of something around my bladder. I was told that I needed to go to a urologist but I can't go because my insurance was cancelled.

*

SHAUNA COX
Shauna was diagnosed with
endometriosis in 2012 at age 29

My very first period, at the age of nine, was abnormally painful. The secretaries at the schools I attended quickly learned my name, as I would be in their office at least once a month to call my parents for permission to go home sick. I would miss one to two days of school per month (the first day or two of my period) because I would be in so much pain from cramping that I would be throwing up. This, combined with diarrhea, and heavy, long periods made my life as an "official woman" as my mom called it, difficult to say the least.

My mom brought me to several doctors, each with a different explanation: I was told that it was normal, that I had dysmenorrhea and to take Advil, and that I had IBS. At the age of fourteen, a doctor finally suggested that I might have endometriosis. I was put on birth control pills (Marvelon) to regulate my cycle and to try to alleviate some of the pain. While it helped a bit with the pain, and did regulate my periods to where I could predict to the day when it was going to start, I was still missing one to two days of school a month and often still vomiting due to the severe cramps that came with every period.

At age sixteen, I went to another doctor who mentioned the possibility of endometriosis but mistakenly believed it could be diagnosed in an ultrasound. When nothing was found, as is often the case, my doctor decided that I didn't have endometriosis. I decided to do my own research and found that the only way to definitively diagnose endometriosis was through a laparoscopy. All of my symptoms seemed to fit the diagnosis and so from that moment on, despite what my latest doctor had said, I saw myself as a woman with probable endometriosis.

Unfortunately, in my research, I also learned that some women with endometriosis suffer from infertility. It has always been my dream to be a mom. I used to want seven kids, that's how badly I wanted to parent! Because I was still young, however, I pushed the fear of never being able to have children to the back of my mind.

When I was in my early twenties, things got a little bit better. I still often had to lie in bed from the pain when on my period, and I would miss one day of work a month, but it wasn't so bad that I was throwing up anymore. My periods were still fairly heavy, though, and I started to have pain with bowel movements when on my period.

In August 2010, two weeks after getting married, my husband and I decided to start trying to get pregnant. I went off the birth control that I had been on for thirteen years. My periods were very abnormal after going off the pill (anywhere from twenty-five to thirty-five days apart) but, strangely, my painful periods actually got better! Advil was generally enough for me, and I was only missing one day of work every three to four months. The bleeding also got quite a bit lighter.

After six months of trying to conceive, my doctor gave me some first line fertility medications to try. When that didn't work, we were referred to a fertility clinic. The fertility doctor decided to operate on me to find out if endometriosis was causing our problems with infertility. I wasn't a stranger to operations! I have had five surgeries (not counting oral surgeries) in the past unrelated to pelvic issues. While this first surgery didn't confirm the diagnosis, a second surgery months later revealed severe endometriosis.

My greatest frustrations related to endometriosis are lack of understanding and expertise in the medical community. There are still so many doctors who say women need a hysterectomy or treat that as cure, when it isn't a cure for endometriosis. In Canada, there is a lack of medical expertise. Our greatest doctors aren't as skilled as many of the doctors in the USA (which are also hard to find), and while our medical care is free, our government won't recognize that some patients need to go elsewhere to find true experts who can give them the best care possible. I am also frustrated that surgery wasn't offered to me at an earlier age when my endometriosis might have been easier to treat and not so far advanced, when I might still have had a better shot at getting pregnant. It's depressing to think that this disease might have taken away my dreams of being a mom, and that if more awareness existed in the medical community, I might have had a shot at those dreams coming true. But I do still have hope! Since my diagnosis, I have found a couple of doctors who may give me the best shot at surgically removing all of the endometriosis, possibly giving me a chance at having children.

*

JORDANNE GOLD
Jordanne was diagnosed with
endometriosis in 2014 at age 22

My endometriosis began suddenly and quietly. I didn't know exactly what was going on, but I knew something was wrong. Menstrual cramps were something I had never experienced while growing up. As an athletic girl, I barely had a period let alone any of the common premenstrual symptoms most women feel. I went through twenty-two years of life being blind to how grateful I should have been. And then things started to change.

In November 2013, being freshly twenty-two years old, there was a shift in my body. My light, almost nonexistent, three-day periods morphed into something I had never experienced. The short twenty-day cycles I was accustomed to jumped to an unexpected thirty-two days, and I had the unsettling feeling that my body was trying to tell me something was wrong. Along with this new cycle length came something else I had never experienced before: severe pelvic pain. Each month brought more confusion along with an underlying feeling that something was wrong. My period was no longer easy, and the pain started to tear apart my life.

Although pain was a large part of what I was dealing with, it was by far not the only thing. Fatigue, nausea, and sacroiliac joint pain also became part of my day-to-day life. The next five months were filled with confusion, agony, and stress that led me to seek help. The mild cramps and pain grew worse as time went on. The pain was no longer an inconvenience, but rather a monster that started to take over. It was unlike anything I had felt before.

The burning pain began in my pelvic cavity and radiated through my body, leaving me unable to move. In turn, this started to affect my school, work, and personal life. Along with the physical changes, I started to feel the constant weight of depression pushing down on me. Life started to feel blurry and the pain convinced me that I didn't want to live through what I was experiencing. The depression, anxiety, and pain started taking over my life.

I began my journey toward finding help by seeing the general practitioner who I'd been seeing for two years. My first appointment ended with my practitioner making me feel as though I was being weak. She made me feel like I was an inconvenience, and that it was not possible for this pain to be happening. When the bloodwork and ultrasound tests returned, it showed a hormone imbalance. I was diagnosed with PCOS, polycystic ovarian disease, and prescribed metformin, an insulin stabilizer, and was told there was nothing else I could do. But three months of taking metformin made no difference in pain. In fact, over those three months I ended up experiencing more pain and good days became fewer and fewer. I saw my original practitioner three more times, each time explaining that I couldn't live in this much pain. Each appointment ended with disappointment, as this doctor brushed off my symptoms as normal and said there was nothing anyone could do for me.

At this point, it had been nine months of confusion and pain with no end in sight. I now found myself in the local emergency room every month. Those doctors urged me to find out what was going on with my body, and I'd try to explain what I had been through for almost a year, but it felt like no one seemed to understand.

I spent the next part of my life jumping from doctor to doctor, desperately trying to find someone who would care. Every doctor I saw gave me the same response as my first practitioner, telling me over and over that menstrual pain was normal. Eventually, after constant emergency trips to the hospital and as my mental health started getting worse and worse, I was referred to a local OB/GYN. We were now a step forward and I truly felt like change was coming; however little did I know I still had a long road ahead of me.

This empathetic and compassionate OB/GYN was a nice change compared to how I had been treated. We ran test after test over the next month, all of which seemed to show inconclusive results. The OB/GYN then explained that there were no answers for me. He explained that I may have something called endometriosis, but that there was no treatment for it and I was too young for surgery.

After that appointment, I decided I was going to take control, I was going to dedicate myself to researching everything I possibly could about endometriosis and to truly understand the monster that was destroying my life. I joined support groups and read every journal article I could find. Through my research, I was able to learn how important excision surgery from an endometriosis specialist was, and which doctors in my province were trained specifically to treat the disease. Once I had the name of a specialist, I went to a walk-in clinic and got a referral the very next day.

Although I had hoped for a doctor who would know what to do with me, the pain was still growing and had now spread to every day, a constant dull ache that made my whole world seem darker. I started feeling pain in my bowels and bladder, and the nausea and fatigue started to intensify. Sometimes I spent the whole day vomiting for what seemed like no reason. The four months it took for me to see my new doctor felt like an eternity, and every day I felt worse.

My first appointment with my new doctor was an emotionally exhausting day. Within the first five minutes, she shared that she suspected I had endometriosis along with adenomyosis, but the wait for surgery was five months. We would have to manage the pain until then. This seemed like an impossible task, but there was nothing else I could do.

My new doctor saw me every month until surgery. As the day of surgery approached, I had never wanted anything more or anything less at the exact same time. After surgery, after all these years, I finally had a physical representation of the pain going on inside of me.

Recovery was longer and harder than I had ever expected. I needed more time off work than planned. By the two-month mark, I felt as though I had lost hope, was strung out on heavy pain killers, and seeing little to no improvement. At five months post procedure, I started having moments when I felt pain-free, a feeling I hadn't experienced in years. As slow and inconspicuous as the pain came, it now was starting to leave. I am now at seven months with my Mirena IUD (along with excision surgery), and I've gained part of my life back. Although endometriosis is still in my life, it no longer controls my life, and I am able to be "me" again.

*

CHRISTA HALL
Christa was diagnosed with
endometriosis in 2015 at age 24

My periods started differently than others. I was a late bloomer, being thirteen when I started my first period. I started out having heavier periods, and thinking that going through a pad an hour was normal.

After two years, my periods became extremely painful. During my first emergency room trip, the doctor refused to believe I was a virgin and said I had to be pregnant. He told me I had cysts.

At the follow up, my primary doctor put me on constant birth control. For two years I went without a typical monthly period. I still bled randomly and would cramp. After losing my virginity, I bled heavily whenever I had sex. I thought that was normal. When I finally saw my first gynecologist, he immediately took me off birth control and my periods came rushing back. He ordered bloodwork and ultra-sounds, and I told him how the pain before my period was horrible.

I had my first surgery in 2009. We now believe the roots hadn't popped through yet, so they couldn't see the endometriosis. Though I did not get an endometriosis diagnosis, my ovaries were covered in cysts, my left ovary was adhered to the back of my uterus, and my intestines down to my bowels were completely covered in scar tissue.

My pain subsided for the most part and I went back on birth control, with a period every month. It wasn't until my husband and I decided to stop the birth control and tried getting pregnant in 2012, when everything became worse. Much, much worse. I was in the emergency room almost every other month in excruciating pain that made me vomit and pass out. I was trying to find a gynecologist who would listen to me, but was told I "just couldn't handle period pains."

When I was in the emergency room, I tried to explain to doctors that my pain seemed to coincide with my periods and ovulation. In August 2013, I met Dr. Morowski in the emergency room, and we spoke of endometriosis again. We decided I would first try six months of Clomid to try to get pregnant. When that didn't work, we reset my reproductive system by chemically inducing menopause through a monthly injection of Lupron. At age twenty-two, I was going through menopause.

My husband and I were married in April 2014, when I had been menopausal for about three months. I decided to stop the injections soon after, as the hot flashes, mood swings, and night sweats along with constant migraines and extreme weight gain were too much.

After finding out my father-in-law had cancer, my husband and I moved from Connecticut to Oklahoma to help take care of his father. Out in Oklahoma, my stress was high and my flares were even higher. After stopping Lupron, my pain became almost constant. Since my husband and I were not working and uninsured, I had to find natural ways to help with pain. My symptoms also got much worse. I could almost never have sex, as it was too painful. Bowel movements became excruciating, and my "endometriosis belly" became almost constant. In January 2015, I had a period so heavy, I went into anemic shock from flooding eight pads in less than seven hours.

We moved back to Virginia Beach in April 2015, and finally got insurance in October. My first thing was to go see a gynecologist. I went back to the office who saw me when I was a teenager, but the doctor was no longer there. My first appointment was scheduled as an annual checkup. I brought up the pain and extremely heavy bleeding. The midwife who saw me said, "Oh, that is normal, but since you've been trying to get pregnant for so long, we recommend a fertility clinic." I was shocked that extreme amounts of pain and bleeding severe enough to cause shock were considered normal by a midwife!

After researching the two fertility clinics in the area, I decided on The New Hope Center. I called and had an appointment within the week. During my first appointment, I told Dr. Robin about my pain and bleeding. I immediately had an ultrasound where they found multiple cysts on my ovaries, that the lining of my uterus was too thick, my uterus filled with polyps, and I had a single fibroid right in the center of my uterus.

On December 3, 2015, I had surgery. They cleared my uterus out, found massive amounts of scar tissue, and stage one endometriosis. Though the adhesions were smaller, there were many throughout the entire pelvis. After years of pain, it was finally confirmed.

My first month after surgery was great! It was decided I would go on birth control until my husband and I finished testing to keep the endometriosis at bay, and then would go off it when we could start trying to conceive again.

In February, I was on two rounds of strong antibiotics and decided not to waste a month of birth control. In March, my husband and I found out I was pregnant, though it was a short lived excitement. I miscarried later that week. At my follow up, we found out that I was in need of another surgery. My left ovary had adhered itself again to the back of my uterus, this time near the cervix. Whenever I stretched my abdomen, my ovary would pull.

I had my third surgery on April 21, 2016. They found more endometriosis along with massive amounts of scar tissue on my bowels and throughout the abdomen. In December 2015, I started physical therapy for chronic pelvic pain management, which has been working out wonderfully.

*

BETH JENSEN
Beth was diagnosed with
endometriosis in 2009 at age 20

My endometriosis story started when I was ten years old. I went home early on the first day of my first period. I actually thought I was dying, as I couldn't remember my mother telling me anything about that kind of pain. I thought it was supposed to be uncomfortable, not actually cause pain. When I think back on it now, I would give anything to go back to that low-pain level.

As I grew up my periods got worse. My mother couldn't seem to fathom the kind of pain I was feeling, though it's not like she had experienced really bad pain. By the time I was turning fourteen, I had been put on multiple antidepressants and ended up missing three months of ninth grade. Those pills made me seriously crazy, I was doing things that were brash and irrational. This directly led to my introduction of intercourse and marijuana, the latter of which I can honestly say saved my life. I stopped taking the antidepressants and started smoking marijuana on the sly, and took Tylenol #1 and Tylenol #3 in an attempt to have a somewhat normal life. This continued for many years, while constantly changing birth controls. By the time I was seventeen, I moved out and was on the search for help, as my pain had gotten worse.

Around age nineteen, I found a family doctor who told me my pain was not normal. She suspected endometriosis and sent me to a gynecologist. At age twenty, the gynecologist performed a laparoscopy and confirmed endometriosis and during this surgery, performed ablation surgery. At my six-week follow-up, he put me on Lupron, telling me it was just hormone therapy. I took this medication. Oh, how I regret both the surgery and the medication.

More time passed and the pain got worse. I found a surgeon who performed excision surgery on me in January 2015. At that six-week follow-up, I was told I had suspected adenomyosis and could try either an IUD or have a hysterectomy. I opted for the IUD but by the end of that year I had more pain, so I was scheduled for a hysterectomy.

Since my hysterectomy, I have felt better even though I still live in daily pain. If I keep myself medicated I can function with a pain level of about four to five every day. But I'll keep fighting for those who love me, and for those I love.

*

JESSICA NOEL
Jessica was diagnosed with
endometriosis in 1991 at age 9

I am thirty-five years old and my battle started over twenty-eight years ago when I collapsed from severe abdominal pains at age seven and was rushed to the emergency room. I waited for sixteen hours for my mom to be told it must have been very bad gas. Tests showed nothing except fluid in my ovaries which they said was normal for my age. I had right sided pain on and off for months.

I started my cycle at age eight years and two months, and was rushed to the emergency room again for heavy bleeding. I was going through an overnight pad every thirty minutes. My mom and I waited eight hours only to be told "Oh, it's just a normal heavy flow," and sent home. I returned the following three days for heavy bleeding and such severe pain that I was blacking out. On the third day I was put in the insanity ward against my mom's permission. The ER doctor believed that everything was in my head and I was making it all up.

My mom and I saw thirty doctors and specialists before we found one who ran a bunch of tests and recommended surgery to determine what was wrong. I had to quit all medications four weeks before surgery. It was the longest four weeks of my young life.

I went in at 6:43 a.m. on January 12, 1991, and came out at 1:27 p.m. I was told at 3:40 p.m. that I had severe stage four endometriosis. My whole right side was covered in lesions and endometriosis. I had a fifteen-centimeter chocolate cyst on my right ovary that was drained and removed. I was told my case was the worst the surgeon had ever seen. If we had waited two more days, I would have lost my ovary.

I was in pain but for the first time in two years it was not severe, and that felt great. I was started on birth control that day and felt great for six months before symptoms started coming back. I went in again for another laparoscopy to remove more endometriosis tissue. I had four more laparoscopies after that.

At age fifteen, I underwent excision surgery which worked great for ten years. But over those ten years, I sadly lost eight pregnancies due to them all attaching to my right side, which has low blood flow.

In total, I have had thirty surgeries for endometriosis. The most recent was June 8, 2014, to remove my appendix which was covered and had a tumor growing in it. I've been on several birth controls, tons of pain medications, and had Lupron treatment three times. Each time was great, but now I'm paying for it with bone and hair loss. I've had fifteen miscarriages total, all before or around fifteen weeks gestation.

I am one of the lucky ones who can still work and function every day. I also have fibromyalgia, irritable bowel syndrome, interstitial cystitis, chronic pain syndrome, chronic fatigue syndrome, and a blood disorder. I take four pain killers three times a day, which is down from nine. I switched from tampons and store-bought pads to cloth pads and a menstrual cup two years ago. I've since noticed a great change in my cycle and pain levels, and saved three thousand dollars a year. I am using more natural stuff to help with my symptoms.

I am on a waiting list to try vaginal streaming which is supposed to have great benefits for the uterus, and I'm trying to eat healthy with hopes of getting pregnant and carrying to term. I haven't yet given up but if I'm not blessed with a little one by age thirty-seven, I'll press to have a hysterectomy. I know this is not a cure, but seeing all I have is my left tube, left ovary, uterus, and cervix, I am at risk for cancer.

I truly hope that in my lifetime they find a cure for endometriosis because this disease has ruined a lot of lives, and has killed too. Plus, no one likes being in pain, nauseous, bloated, dizzy, and bleeding clots the size of Texas. I am very lucky I have a great support system of my mom, sister, fiancé, and endometriosis sisters worldwide.

*

CARMELA POLLOCK
Carmela was diagnosed with
endometriosis in 1995 at age 25

My journey with endometriosis and the pain I carried for many years drove me to create a new life from the pieces of the old. Endometriosis taught me the extent of my resilience and courage to push through a sometimes debilitating disease. It tested my resolve through the many misdiagnoses and the label of hypochondria.

I believe my endometriosis began in my early twenties. Monthly pain and heavy bleeding were common, and I thought that was normal for most women. Seeing it from a generalist perspective and to avoid concerning family or friends, I trained myself to redirect the conversation if someone was to comment on how unwell I looked. I was tired of hearing "See a doctor," when all they had done up to that point was recommend over-the-counter pain relief that didn't work.

It was 1995 and I was twenty-five years old. I was alone and woke to the most debilitating pain that left me unable to walk. The bed sheets were covered in blood. I was fatigued and consumed with pain that engulfed my entire body. I called the ambulance service and was rushed to a local hospital where I was attended to immediately. I was hemorrhaging, in agony, scared and confused. That night changed my life and forced me to rethink my position on "keeping quiet." Some days later I was officially diagnosed with endometriosis, a ruptured cyst on the left ovary and several fibroids.

And so the road to understanding began. This period in my life brought great relief, knowing that I wasn't a hypochondriac. However, it also brought with it sorrow, receiving news from my gynecologist that conceiving and carrying a child to full term would be near impossible due to the condition of my uterus and ovaries. I recall feeling grief for the first time—an ambiguous loss. In time, I refused to accept the possibility of being childless and made sure it didn't undermine the relationship I had with my husband.

Over the years, I underwent a number of procedures to control the endometriosis. It was relentless and not much changed in relation to my condition. The pain was persistent but I carried on with grace and lived in hope that something would help. I embraced alternative therapies and combined them with western medicine. I never gave up on finding the way to free myself from endometriosis.

In 2006, my miracle child was born. Despite the news delivered to me ten years earlier, he represented that I am, indeed, the creator of my story. He is a tangible representation of the growth and tenacity of my spirit, regardless of the diagnosis. He is a gift I treasure every day. Following the birth of my son, the years ensuing challenged me on many levels. Trying to juggle the fatigue of being a new mum, working, and also supporting a husband suffering from depression, my reserves of energy were depleted. Stress took control of my life. I now believe that the effects of stress can be directly attributed to the many years of menstrual pain and recurring endometriosis. I tried a number of alternative therapies and medical procedures, with little or sometimes no long-term success. I came to a fork in the road where I needed to make a decision to improve my life, and bring it back to wholeness that was sustainable and consistent. I had reached my forties and was aged beyond my years, and so this triggered the next phase in my endometriosis journey.

The decision to have a hysterectomy was not one I accepted lightly. After several weeks of self-analysis and deep soul work, I recognized that my heart was wounded and my body needed to rest and repair from the endometriosis fight. The gynecologist made it very clear that the procedure may not stop the endometriosis, but I had to make a conscious effort to bring wellness back into my vocabulary. This was my last resort, and I played all my cards to bring health back home to my tired body.

It has been six years since my hysterectomy. I am grateful for the pain-free life without endometriosis. The operation gifted me a freedom to rejoice in my feminine aspects rather than dread the monthly change. It also revealed the need to slow down and respect life in quiet contemplation and expression, in pursuing self-inquiry, self-exploration and self-discovery. Freedom from pain and the resulting preservation of the mind, body and spirit, is my right.

On reflection, I consider my physical pain to be a representation of my emotions. If I had an emotional reaction, I felt it lodged in my abdomen. How do I know this? In my twenties I worked and played hard. With an active social life and strong work commitment, I made little time to simply breathe and just be. Stress levels were high as I worked long hours to build a career and make my mark in a male-dominated industry. Politics and sexual discrimination were commonplace and being a sensitive person, I felt it all. This carried through into my thirties. Coupled with all this, I had unexplored and denied emotions stored in my body from childhood and broken relationships that scarred me deeply.

I saw the hysterectomy as the outward mechanism to start my healing, as the endometriosis represented a vast reservoir of pain I had neglected to address. Circumstances also demanded I turn inward to understand the trinity—mind, body and spirit—to do the deeper work. Through mindfulness, energy healing, and daily journaling, I healed those parts the hysterectomy could not.

I pen my journey for this book to acknowledge the past and accept with love the hard fight that is endometriosis. I also take comfort that life can be more than a disease, but a library of beautiful lessons ready for us to uncover and learn.

*

ASHLEY ROMANKO
Ashley was diagnosed with
endometriosis in 2005 at age 21

I started experiencing symptoms when I got my first period at age sixteen. It was painful, but I was told that was normal. I just continued with life because the pain wasn't bad. I was irregular and wanted to go on birth control because I heard it regulates your period. The last thing I wanted was to suddenly get my period one day in school. Most of the time I had to sit out during Phys Ed. Eventually I got sick of the judgmental stares and stopped going to class.

During my teen years, every month was painful but at least I knew when it was coming. I was always told that cramps are supposed to be painful. It was hard to do normal activities, but was told it was good to continue normal activities during my period. It was hard to concentrate on school or anything else. I later learned that I could take continuous birth control and skip my period! A few years passed and things worsened. The pain became daily and was excruciating. I went to doctor after doctor but was told, "Take some Tylenol and just rest," or "You're too stressed. Here's some clonazepam," or "You're fine."

I went to the emergency room in excruciating pain but all the tests came back normal. I was finally referred to a gynecologist who, at the very first appointment, suspected endometriosis. I had no idea what that was, but was relieved that he was actually trying to help. I was booked for laparoscopic surgery, which is the only way to get a diagnosis. Endometriosis doesn't show up in any other test.

While I waited for surgery, I was given strong pain medications. I went to the pain specialist and had an assessment, physiotherapy, biofeedback, and group therapy. I found that the biofeedback helped the most.

Finally, surgery day came and confirmed that I had endometriosis. The doctor said that if I wanted children, we should start trying now because endometriosis can cause infertility. My husband and I discussed this and decided that we did want children. I was twenty-three years old when I got pregnant. During the pregnancy, I had awful morning sickness and the pain was still there. I had labor complications and needed blood transfusions and a D/C surgery. I guess some of the placenta got stuck and my uterus wouldn't close. It was a pretty painful experience but at least I got a little baby out of it.

The pain continued. It's hard to raise a child with chronic pelvic and low back pain. I had another laparoscopic surgery around 2009. My favorite part of surgery is being knocked out by the anesthesia, because then I don't feel pain. The worst part is waking up by a nurse yelling your name. I realize the nurse is expected to do this, but it sure startles you and then just makes you cranky.

A few years later we decided we would like another child. Our son was born in 2011. I'm very lucky that I didn't have trouble conceiving although I struggled during both pregnancies and labors.

I felt very alone and started searching for online support groups. I found a couple and started connecting with other women like me! Other women who feel exactly how I feel! Who knows what the pain feels like. It was very uplifting and amazing to find this kind of connection, where another being actually feels what you are feeling! We will continue to advocate for one another and every other woman who is dealing with this awful disease.

I then went to another doctor who prescribed Visanne. It made me feel crazy. I had massive hair loss, sweats, severe psychotic mood, headaches, and was still in pain. I stayed on it for about six months, hoping for a change. It didn't help me but it has helped others.

I was booked for another surgery, but this time it was excision surgery. I was so excited because excision done by an endometrial specialist is the gold standard for removal. It will help if it's done right. Finally the surgery date came and I was put under. When I woke up, imagine my surprise when the doctor told me she did ablation (burning the disease) rather than excision (ripping it out by its roots). I was so disgusted with her and if I would have known she was going to do that, I would have waited for someone more experienced.

*

SAYDA WYMER
Sayda was diagnosed with
endometriosis in 2010 at age 35

I began experiencing pain in 2000, but was not properly diagnosed. I remember having very heavy periods and severe cramps but nothing could be done. For many years I dealt with pain and heavy bleeding without knowing why. I thought maybe it was just me who had heavy periods.

One day while working on the ship, I received a call from the gynecologist who said I needed to come to the hospital due to an abnormal pap smear, so I did. Little did I know, that moment was going to change the rest of my life.

The doctor told me I had precancerous cells growing in my cervix, and she needed to remove half of it. All of it was done with a laser, and she sent me on my way. I could barely walk from the pain. She hadn't numbed the area, much less give anything for pain. Not even Tylenol. I remember that day like it was yesterday. I was deployed the following day.

About a month later, I went to the ship's sick call and was airlifted to Bahrain. From there, I spent two months at the base waiting to stop bleeding. Once the bleeding stopped, I went back to the ship and continued my job. Ever since then I've battled heavy periods and was told that once I had a baby, I would be okay. I married my husband the week I got back. I had been told I could never have kids, so I wasn't on contraception, and to my surprise I got pregnant. By 2009, I couldn't handle the pain and went to the doctor who immediately said, "I think you have endometriosis. I'm going to refer you to a gynecologist."

In May 2010, I had my first surgery and was told I had stage four endometriosis. The surgery alleviated a lot of the pain and bleeding, but five years later it was time for another. By May 2015, I didn't feel like it did much. So here I am stuck with the bloat and pain again.

*

JACQUIE YOUNG
Jacquelyn was diagnosed with
endometriosis in 2012 at age 22

My experience with endometriosis started when I was eight years old. I started my period that summer, and woke to find my underwear covered in brown. I called to my mom because I wasn't sure what was happening. She sat me down and explained that I had gotten my period and what to expect. She then said, "Welcome to womanhood!"

For me, it wasn't an event to celebrate. I felt disgusted by the nausea and pain. I didn't want to be a woman—I was eight! I got through that horrible first period, hoping that the discomfort was just my body adjusting to the new changes. Turns out that the nausea, pain and vomiting would return every month. Luckily once my period stopped, so did the pain. The problem back then was that I missed three to four days of school each month because of severe pain. My mom thought it was normal because she experienced the same thing.

When I was fifteen, my first real endometriosis pain happened. I had a sharp pain in my lower right side. I went to the school nurse and she thought it was my appendix rupturing. I went to the hospital and they said it was just an ovarian cyst. Years after that first episode, I found myself constantly having ovarian cysts and at times thinking it was my appendix. In my early twenties, sex hurt so badly that I'd be in bed the next day. I finally went to see an OB/GYN for right-sided pain. I was twenty-two when the doctor did an exam and said, "You're too young to have endometriosis," and sent me to the hospital for an outpatient CT scan, thinking my appendix was to blame for this pain. I went for the scan and it turns out that I'm allergic to the IV contrast. I went into anaphylactic shock and they had to revive me. But guess what? No appendicitis. No answers. No nothing.

I saw a new doctor after moving from Pennsylvania to Boston to be with my future husband. I was diagnosed with endometriosis at age twenty-two. By that point, my pain had become chronic. It persisted after surgery so I sought help elsewhere. It was extremely difficult to have great care when there are so few specialists in the United States. The only way to effectively treat endometriosis is to have a specialist excise the disease. Each time I saw a general gynecologist, they would burn off the surface and leave the deeper disease inside.

I was so frustrated with being let down, downplayed by doctors, and just sick of being sick. I was a guinea pig with medications. The side effects were so awful, almost worse than my normal symptoms. I became too sick to work and had to leave my dream job at Sephora to focus on getting better. I went broke from copays, prescriptions and parking for all these appointments. It's so expensive, and the money lost from not working was tough to deal with.

By the time I was twenty-three, I was in a pain clinic with people much older than me. I had nerve blocks and steroid injections to try to rid this horrible pain. One time, the nerve block worked for two days and it was amazing to feel somewhat normal. But I had to leave the pain clinic because the doctor said there was still endometriosis deep inside, and treating the surface wouldn't give me much benefit.

I've been going to pelvic floor physical therapy for almost a year now. It's helped tremendously with the muscle spasms and tightness. I also finally found an amazing endometriosis specialist who does excision surgery. I had my appendix removed during one surgery because of all the false alarms. Turns out it was covered with endometriosis and on the verge of rupturing. I've had a total of nine surgeries in the last three years.

This disease can be very isolating at times. You feel so many emotions. Anger. Why am I sick? Why me? Those are the questions I used to ask myself. I would dream of my old life when I wasn't sick. But the reality is I'll never go back to who I used to be even if I get well again. Too much has happened. I'm stronger now, so how could I ever be the same? I'm a new version of myself and no longer mourn the loss of my old life.

I've met some incredible people on this endometriosis journey, women just like me who have earned their battle scars. Being sick isn't a positive thing, but I try to make it that way. How would I have met half my friends if I had never experienced this? How would I gain such compassion if I've never suffered? These are all blessings in disguise. I truly believe everything happens for a reason.

*

JENNIFER YOUNG
Jennifer was diagnosed with
endometriosis in 2009 at age 21

My symptoms began at age twelve when I had my first period, although I wasn't fully diagnosed until several years later. Every month the pain ranged from complete torture all the way to utter hell. I had a very heavy flow the first three days, sometimes four, and filled a pad almost every hour. Those first three days the pain would be so horrible that I couldn't get out of bed or keep anything down. I would roll around crying and begging my mom to take the pain away. My heating pad quickly became my best friend but that, combined with pain medicine, worked only half the time. I was put on a merry-go-round of different birth control medicines to try to help.

Every month was a repeat of the previous month. There was no rhyme or reason to the pattern. This continued until I turned eighteen, when more symptoms started showing up. I was at work one day. My position wasn't a strenuous one—I worked at BJ's Wholesale Club in loss prevention where I would check receipts against items in the members' carts at the door. I was in between members and had stooped down to pick something off the floor when the pain started. It was a milder pain in my lower right side. Over the next few minutes, the pain progressively got worse. A member quickly offered to get my manager who took one look, saw the sweat pouring off me, and called my parents. They rushed me to my doctor who was very concerned it was my appendix, as it hurt when she pushed down. She sent me straight to the hospital for a contrast CT scan and ultrasound. The results came back as a ruptured ovarian cyst, and I was told I had more on the other side that would likely rupture as well. Unfortunately, the only thing that could be done for them would be to take prescription pain medication.

The random rupturing cysts continued until I turned twenty-one and developed a cyst on my left ovary that did not rupture. This time the cyst grew. I had many trips to the emergency room over that cyst, thinking that my ovary had to be inverting and causing all the pain and nausea. When it became obvious that this cyst was not going to disappear by itself, the doctor became concerned that this was cancer and referred me to a local gynecological-oncologist.

This doctor also suspected endometriosis, and told me at my first appointment that he wanted to see what the cyst was going to do over the span of a month or so. When it didn't disappear within the ideal timeframe, we agreed on surgery to remove it by laparoscopy. Once he got inside my abdomen, he discovered that it wasn't a cyst, but a baseball-sized tumor inside my left ovary. He almost couldn't save the ovary because of the way he had to remove the tumor. He sent the tumor straight to pathology for testing while I was still in surgery. The results came back benign.

At my postop appointment, the doctor said the endometriosis was very severe, and I had an extremely low chance of being able to carry a baby to full term, or even getting pregnant. I was heartbroken, and immediately started asking for a hysterectomy. I didn't see the point in continuing painful periods if I wasn't going to be able to have kids. My request was denied due to my age, but now I am glad.

In 2012, I found out that a miracle occurred. I was pregnant with our daughter! I carried her full term, but had a very rough and painful pregnancy, and an even tougher delivery due to a car accident at thirty-nine weeks. We almost lost her and she was born by emergency Cesarean section after I would not dilate past three centimeters. She was nine months old when I learned I was again pregnant, this time with our son. He was born in 2015. He was also a very rough pregnancy and I started miscarrying him at twenty weeks. I was pretty much on modified bed rest until he was born also via Cesarean section. My doctor said that if I got pregnant again, my body would not be able to handle it, and one or both of us would not make it. I made the choice to have my tubes tied at the same time as my son's birth.

After each pregnancy, my endometriosis got worse. I started to bleed longer and heavier during periods. I started to wish again that I could just have everything taken out. Family and friends were also asking me why I wasn't having it done. I explained that I didn't think they would do it for me, even though my tubes had been tied. I had just kind of accepted that this would not happen in my case.

Finally, after a trip to my family doctor for a suspected urinary tract infection earlier this year, I explained that I hadn't found a new doctor since moving here. I felt like I had gotten worse and asked if she would refer me to one. Within two days, my new doctor called with an appointment date for two weeks later. At that appointment, after listening to my medical and family history and current problems, he did an internal ultrasound and pap smear. It was discovered that I had cysts on both ovaries. He gave me three options. I could do the Lupron shot since I had stopped reacting to birth control (I said no). I could have the cysts removed along with as much of the endometrial tissue as he could, or I could have a complete hysterectomy and remove everything including uterus, tubes, ovaries and cervix. Originally, I asked to have the cysts removed but called back the next day asking instead for the hysterectomy.

I had surgery on April 28. While I know it's not a cure for my endometriosis, it did take care of the adenomyosis that I didn't know I had because I was never diagnosed with it. With that being said, I am just thankful every day when I wake up pain-free and period-free until the endometriosis rears its ugly head again, but hopefully it never will.

*

Every rainbow begins with rain.
-UNKNOWN

*

CHAPTER TWO

Describing the Pain

"Yes, hello, I'd like a refund on my body. It's kinda defective and really expensive." -ENDOBODY

Living with endometriosis means pain. Some days it's better, some days it's worse. Some days it requires medical attention to manage. Because pain is an invisible symptom, it can be difficult to describe. Is it stabbing? Dull and aching? Is it constant or intermittent?

*

ADRIEANNE BEASLEY
Adrieanne was diagnosed with
endometriosis in 2014 at age 31

My pain from my endometriosis occurs almost every day. There are some days when I can barely get out of bed. The pain affects my activities, and when it is really bad I cannot go to the gym or do any physical activity. On good days the pain is mild pelvic and lower abdominal cramping. On my worst days, the pain is extreme cramping in my lower abdomen and pelvic area. It is a sharp shooting pain that can travel all the way down my thighs. My lower back is very sore and I cannot even stand straight. The pain is not as bad since having an IUD placed, as I no longer get periods, however it still can be pretty excruciating. I have an anti-inflammatory medication that can sometimes help to take the edge off, however I am currently exploring better options for pain control.

*

SHILOH BRITT
Shiloh was diagnosed with
endometriosis in 2011 at age 22

There really wasn't much pain at all to begin with, just irregularities when I would have severe cramping around the time of my period, or when I would bleed for an excessive amount of time, or not at all. As time wore on, the cramping became more commonplace and more severe. By the time I was twenty-one, the pain manifested as jabbing and white-hot pain in my lower abdomen. My legs and lower back would go numb and the pelvic pain would be so intense that it would bring tears to my eyes and send me to the floor in pain, with me even occasionally losing consciousness. I would develop migraines, and all-over body aches to accompany this. My level of fatigue was so much that even a short walk took all the energy I had. I was bloated all the time, to the point that I looked pregnant. In the two years before my surgery, these days became a weekly occurrence. The final month before my surgery, I was mostly bedridden and relied on oxycodone and heating pads to keep the pain from consuming me.

An excerpt from my journal:

There are days I can't get out to nature. There are days I can't get out of bed. Not figuratively, as in a constant depressed state. There are days when the pain is so striking that I literally can't get out of bed. And yet these are the days when I need nature most. I don't know if this constitutes as a nature journal entry, but it's the time thus far this year when I have had the most closeness with nature—and not being able to physically enjoy it.

It's so beautiful outside today. Sigh. The perfect day to sit outside and write in the nature I so love. One of our kitties, DuneBug, sits in my bedroom window and looks out our second story window at the beautiful day. He casts his little pudgy bob-tailed kitty silhouette across the room, shielding my eyes momentarily from the bright sun streaming though my dingy window. I long to be able to go out and enjoy this delightful day. To be able to sit with the ants and hum with the insects flying around me. I wish to mimic the gulls and scan the sound for seals—always silently wishing for a member of one of the resident orca (J or I maybe, even the elusive K?) pods to make a cameo appearance. I would settle for a quiet walk around my sunny neighborhood. I would love to gaze at the lights dancing in the yards of the many stained-glass windows on my route to the little bench in the quiet park by the sea. I would ponder over the greenery that's taken over some of the old unkempt sheds. Marvel at nature reclaiming what was all along hers. I would enjoy nothing more than to sit with my pen, scrawl in my journal—let the beautiful words wash over me.

Sigh. "Here kitty kitty." Sigh.

Today I tried. I honestly and truly did. I got up, determined, put on my comfy berks (with the socks my husband hates) and put on my flowy endometriosis dress—the one that is loose enough to not make the pain worse with constrictions. I avoided the mirror in the hall. I didn't need reminded of how "pregnant" I looked, I know all too well. I walked determined past the medicine cabinet, out the door (careful not to let any of the "kids" out), and down the steep steps. I got into my car and drove to the park. Got out of my car, took a few steps toward my bench, book and pen in tow….then…then…collapsed. My mind gave out, my legs with it. The nausea hit. I grabbed the car door handle and held myself up…sat down in my car… and cried. I cried. I cried for being so close. I cried out in pain. I cried because all along I somehow knew I should have listened to my body and stayed in bed. I cried because my husband was right—I DO need to take care of myself. And I cried because I was alone. I know my body, know when I need to sleep off a flare up. And yet I have this stubborn idea that maybe it's mind over matter. Maybe if I ignore the pain it will go away. Pain is all in the head anyway. Maybe if I say "I'm fine," then I will be. Maybe if I lie… But I know the truth—and I hate it. I take the long way back to our duplex. I take the streets that I can easily pull to the side of. I drive slow, and put all my energy into concentrating on driving.

So here I am lying in bed with topical warming Tiger Balm smothered on my pelvic and lower back. I feel the Vicodin taking my mind. I hate myself for taking it. I hate the way it makes me feel, but it's a momentary escape from the inescapable pain, and will dull the nausea I get when the pain has gone too far. The pain dulling….I cry once more now. I want my mom, I want my husband, and I want a cure. But there is no one but me. No option but pain management. Even my three cats are nowhere to be found… but there is the sun…

"Things go up and down. If you can survive the down, it will come back." –John Denver

*

EMMA CLIFTON
Emma was diagnosed with
endometriosis in 2015 at age 30

My pain changes from month to month. It can occur midcycle some months and always during my period. During the midcycle pain, I can generally manage it through heat packs and yoga. However, during my period there is always one, sometimes two days when I have to take pain killers, usually codeine and ibuprofen. It can debilitate me for one full day during my cycle, most months. If I also end up with a migraine, then I end up having to take two days off from work. Prior to having a laparoscopy, the pain was definitely worse, particularly the midcycle pain and stitch-like feeling I would get in my right side, which was also the pain I got during sex.

*

SHANDI CLOUSE
Shandi was diagnosed with
endometriosis in 2015 at age 27

Before my hysterectomy, the pain was constant and for nearly six months it left me completely incapacitated; I spent most days curled up in my chair because moving around just made it worse. My cycles were going on average about twenty days and the pain was there even when I wasn't having my cycle, which in turn caused a lot of intimacy problems in my marriage and in general at home because I just couldn't function. Since my hysterectomy, the flares are frequent and sporadic. I only had the two-month period to heal when the pain subsided. Even still, when I flare up, it can be just as devastating as it was beforehand. First it's the migraine and waves of nausea; it's like a jackhammer in my head and my stomach flops over. The bloating follows soon after, and when the pain hits it's like hot knives in my abdomen, radiating into my lower back and legs, almost like it's tearing from the inside. It's difficult to sit or stand for more than a few minutes and can be so intense that it literally brings me to my knees. On the really bad days, all I can do is lay in bed on my heating pad and wait it out, though that only does so much to relieve it. Sometimes it's just a few hours, if I'm lucky, but more often than not it's unrelenting and will go on for days or weeks on end. At its worst, it's absolutely debilitating; even sleeping is near impossible, even though I'm so exhausted I can barely keep my eyes open.

It's been a little over a year since my symptoms started. So far, the only things I've found that even remotely helps the pain is using heat on my lower back and abdomen, and keeping my stress level down. I'm prescribed Norco for a cervical spinal injury and arthritis, but none of my specialists have attempted to treat the endometriosis pain. On really horrible days, Norco doesn't even come close to relieving it.

*

PATRICIA CONNELLY
Patricia was diagnosed with
endometriosis in 2014 at age 33

Constant pain, stabbing pains in the lower stomach that go around to my back and down my legs. It's starting to go up to my stomach, like when I had my gallbladder taken out.

*

SHAUNA COX
Shauna was diagnosed with
endometriosis in 2012 at age 29

"My pain," as I often refer to it, varies from day to day, week to week, month to month, and apparently year to year. No two days are alike. There are some commonalities, however. My pain is mostly in my lower pelvis, and often worse on the left side. Sometimes it radiates to my back and down my right thigh.

When I was younger, I was only in pain when I was on my period. Day one was by far the worst, but days two and three could be pretty bad as well. I had such severe cramping that I often came home from school vomiting, and had to curl up in a ball in bed, moaning from the agony I was in.

It wasn't until a few years ago that my pain started occurring at other days during the month. In fact, for a while, my pain was worse on days when I wasn't on my period!

The pain itself varies from a dull cramping to sharp, constant pain, to dull with the occasional sharp twinges here and there. Most of the time, I'm able to make it through the day without anyone noticing how I'm feeling inside. Sometimes, however, no matter how hard I try, I can't help crying out, moaning or screaming. It's as if my body takes over and tries to release some of the tension inside.

There are a couple strategies I've learned to help ease the pain. When lying down, I stretch my body as much as I can. I reach my toes out and arch my back until I'm fully stretched, and stay that way for as long as I can. I have no idea why it works; perhaps it helps because it's allowing my organs that are stuck together through adhesions to find a more comfortable position. Or maybe it alleviates the pain briefly for the simple fact that my mind is distracted in the process of stretching.

Heat from a bath is another strategy that works momentarily. I'll draw a bath (or my saint of a husband will draw one for me) as hot as my skin can tolerate, so hot that my legs turn red as soon as they enter the water, and I sometimes need to wait before I can submerge the rest of myself. Once in, I make sure my belly is covered in the water, and I relax all my muscles, closing my eyes and letting my mind wander away from my pain. I guess this strategy is the opposite of the first. Like the stretching exercise, however, the hot bath only works for so long before I have to get out and try something else.

Advil is a given when I'm on my period, and at other times of the month as well. When all else fails, Tylenol #3 will alleviate the pain so that I can either work or sleep, whichever is needed at the time.

*

JORDANNE GOLD
Jordanne was diagnosed with
endometriosis in 2014 at age 22

The pain has changed dramatically over the years. It starts as slight cramps during menstruation and grows in to chronic daily pain. At my worst, the pain during my periods felt like a sharp, burning pain that spread down to reach my toes. This pain often left me bedridden, unable to walk or talk. The best way I can explain the pain is by calling it the worst pain I had ever experienced, pain I never could have imagined. At the start of my journey, I coped by using a heating pad and taking as many pain killers as I could. Since getting symptoms under control, I now have narcotics to take if I feel I need them.

*

CHRISTA HALL
Christa was diagnosed with
endometriosis in 2015 at age 24

Before a flare fully comes on, my chronic fatigue becomes more intense, and I get pressure that makes my organs feel like there's not enough space in my lower abdomen. Then the pain gradually grows until it feels like a red-hot fire poker that's stabbing into my stomach and lower abdomen, pulling and searing my insides. Before my second surgery in December 2015, my pain was near constant. The first day of my cycle (first day of menstruation) was the worst of it. By the time the pain started to somewhat dissipate, I would ovulate and everything started all over again.

Since my surgeries, I use birth control to help control the pain as well as natural and homeopathic ways to help cope such as yoga and meditation, essential oils and herbal teas. If it becomes too much to handle or my coping mechanisms aren't working, I call my doctors to get narcotics as a last resort. I've become used to the frequent pain, and endometriosis doesn't debilitate me as much as it did before. Because of the inflammation that this disease causes, I've developed sciatica, so on average my daily pain is about a three to four on the pain scale. It's usually when I'm flaring that I have a hard time being able to do work or to get anything done.

*

BETH JENSEN
Beth was diagnosed with
endometriosis in 2009 at age 20

My pain has fluctuated over the years. In my early teens it was mostly really bad cramps and I was advised to take Tylenol #1 for the worst pelvic pain. Throughout my teens the pain got worse. The Tylenol #1 stopped helping so I was moved to Tylenol #3, which still barely helped. I was often bedridden with so much pain that I could no longer keep food down for three to five days every month.

Nearing the end of my teens I was prescribed Percocet which eventually led to Demerol. I started missing a lot of work. I was still in pain and the narcotics gave me blinding headaches and intense nausea; nothing helped the way it should. The pain got so bad that I started to lose feeling in my left leg. It was white-hot, like thousands of knives stabbing me and twisting. It radiated through my pelvis going all the way around to my back. This pain made me so nauseous that I literally couldn't eat anything. Sometimes I ate nothing but saltines and water. That was my daily struggle in 2015. Since surgery in November 2015, and having a major medication change, most days my pain has become less blinding. On bad days, I'm right back to where I was before.

*

JESSICA NOEL
Jessica was diagnosed with
endometriosis in 1991 at age 9

I'm in pain around the clock, and have been for twenty-eight years. I'm one of the lucky ones, you can say, because I can still work while in pain. I am mostly at a five out of ten on the pain scale, but I have days when all I do is stay in bed with a heating pad, heated blanket and hot water bottle and pray the pain will lessen. My coping tools are a heating pad, heated blanket, hot water bottle, and hot bath. I use Netflix, coloring books, and reading books to try to keep my mind off the pain. My pain has lessened some since having excision surgery two years ago, but it's starting to come back—worse than before—which is why I am going to ask about scheduling another surgery.

*

CARMELA POLLOCK
Carmela was diagnosed with
endometriosis in 1995 at age 25

If I was given a dollar every time a doctor asked me to describe my pain, I would be a wealthy woman! I started experiencing pain in my twenties. Most people said my pain was normal. However, in subsequent years, the pain became more and more debilitating. It felt like there was a monster with razorlike claws scratching from the inside. No matter which way I sat, lay or stood, it ravaged my abdomen and sent stabbing pains along my lower back and down my legs. The pain would rise and fall, keeping me breathless. At times I found myself gasping for air, because I had developed the coping mechanism of holding my breath as the pain rolled over me. Eventually, the pain was all encompassing and it hurt to move, even to breathe.

Over the years, the chronic nature of endometriosis left a deep emotional wound. No matter how much medical advice I received or medication I took, the sharp clawed endometriosis monster would visit each month, leaving pain and fatigue in its wake.

*

ASHLEY ROMANKO
Ashley was diagnosed with
endometriosis in 2005 at age 21

I have severe debilitating and excruciating pelvic pain daily. It feels like I'm being stabbed repeatedly inside my pelvis, and the knife is being twisted and turned. It feels like acid is being poured on my pelvis and lower back. On my worst days, the pain is all over my pelvis and lower back. It feels like a knife twisting inside and stabbing me repeatedly. The pain increases with ovulation, menstruation, intercourse, stress, and when I stand for long periods. I use an electric heating pad and pain medications to soothe the pain. Keeping my stress down and mindfulness help. I find using my electric heating pad and keeping my mind off the pain with a show can really help stabilize me. When I'm out, sometimes I use disposable heat pads. I'm currently in the process of trying medical marijuana; I've been told it helps many.

*

SAYDA WYMER
Sayda was diagnosed with
endometriosis in 2010 at age 35

My endometrial pain is always there. Some days are better than others. It's not just my lower abdomen that hurts, it's my lower back as well. When I have a flare, I feel as if I have severe menstrual cramps along with lower back pain. The only pain I have felt similar to it was when I was in labor with my first son. There is pressure in the vagina as if a baby is trying to make its way out. Sometimes I double over and rock myself, crying from the pain. It's very intense and overwhelming, as well as anxiety provoking.

Sometimes I start bleeding during the flares. My doctor has me on a Mirena IUD as treatment. I haven't had a period in six years but I spot a few times a month when in severe pain. As I type this, I'm in excruciating pain and have been for the past two weeks. My ovaries feel like they are on fire and my belly feels bloated and stuffed. I go through this several times a month. Some days I'm bedridden because it drains me and all I want to do is sleep and not move. Endometriosis is very painful for me and being in pain every day is part of my daily living. I am never not in pain.

Other organs in my belly hurt as well. Just out of nowhere, I get sharp stabbing pains in other parts of my belly, like under my ribs on the right side. It feels as if I have a sharp fork poking at my liver. I get nauseous and exhausted.

*

JACQUIE YOUNG
Jacquelyn was diagnosed with
endometriosis in 2012 at age 22

My endometrial pain is usually always on my right side. It is sharp, stabbing and gnawing. It feels like cinderblocks repeatedly hitting raw blisters. Endometriosis is a pain that demands to be felt. It started when I was nine years old. I had just started my period and the pain was excruciating. My mother understood because she had also experienced the same pain while growing up. It was so paralyzing that I missed two to three days of school every month. Luckily, after my period ended, so did the pain.

At age twenty, the pain went from once a month to daily. I'm now twenty-six, so that's six years of daily pain. Something shifted in my body and I started having joint pains, stabbing pelvic pain, nausea, diarrhea and just overall did not feel well. Within months of feeling this newfound pain, I was forced to drop out of college because I couldn't get out of bed.

Every day my pain is a baseline of a seven on the pain scale. Every night I go to sleep with my heating pad on the highest setting. Heat is one of the things that really helps soothe the pain. I also take nausea medication and anti-inflammatories, do deep breathing and physical therapy to manage symptoms, and have a Mirena IUD to help manage period pain.

*

JENNIFER YOUNG
Jennifer was diagnosed with
endometriosis in 2009 at age 21

The pain was there every day. It could vary from day to day or even throughout the day on how much I would feel it.

I would use my heating pad all the time as well as lots of pain medicine. I didn't have prescription medicine most of the time, so I would take as much as 2,000 mg at one time of whatever we had, be it Aleve, Advil, Motrin—whatever I could get my hands on at the time, and pray it would take the pain to a somewhat manageable level so I could actually have a conversation with someone.

The other thing I would do was take lots of hot showers. I would turn the water as hot as I could get it and stand under it until the water turned cold. My process was to take medicine and then hop in the shower so by the time I got out, the medicine hopefully would be working at that point, and then I would use the heating pad. Some days my cramping would be so bad, especially during my period, that I had a hard time standing up straight. With each of my pregnancies, the endometriosis definitely got worse.

*

People who need help sometimes look
a lot like people who don't need help.
GLENNON MELTON

*

CHAPTER THREE

Learning the Diagnosis

Warning: I'm having one of those "I don't know which part of my body to cry about first" days.
-ENDOBODY

One research study conducted by the Endometriosis Institute revealed that diagnosis and treatment of endometriosis is delayed by an average of six years from the beginning of symptoms. For some, the diagnosis comes far later. How did your diagnosis come about? And when?

*

ADRIEANNE BEASLEY
Adrieanne was diagnosed with
endometriosis in 2014 at age 31

I was diagnosed with stage four endometriosis by a gynecologist when I was thirty-one years old. When I was given a diagnosis, I was actually relieved to know what I had and that I wasn't going crazy. I did have mixed emotions as well. I was angry that no one had believed me prior to this diagnosis, and that I was treated for everything from depression to hormonal imbalances. I'm glad that I received a proper diagnosis, but wish that there was better treatment for the disease.

*

SHILOH BRITT
Shiloh was diagnosed with
endometriosis in 2011 at age 22

In hindsight, my endometriosis probably started when I was around sixteen. At that point, it was nothing more than usual period pains. Since I was young and had a habit of exaggerating, my parents and doctor thought nothing of it at the time. When I was twenty, we realized something was wrong, but each doctor seemed to have a different idea, none of which were endometriosis. As ridiculous as it sounds, even in 2010, endometriosis was a diagnosis many doctors were unfamiliar with and skeptical of, at best. When I was twenty-two, I ended up in the emergency room with what was diagnosed as a urinary tract infection, bladder infection, pelvic inflammatory disease, and irritable bowel syndrome—all at the same time. In retrospect, this was likely the onset of the beginning of endometriosis flare ups. It would be two more years, and tens of doctors, before we would even hear the term endometriosis. I ponder all the medications I took for years for the wrong thing, and wonder how much time, money, and personal pain could have been saved by a quicker diagnosis.

*

EMMA CLIFTON
Emma was diagnosed with
endometriosis in 2015 at age 30

I was fourteen when I was diagnosed with irritable bowel syndrome but I'm convinced it has always been endometriosis, as the symptoms have remained the same from this age onward, they just varied over the years. I was officially diagnosed at age thirty when I finally had a laparoscopy. I was upset, and almost relieved at the same time. When I woke from surgery, my gynecologist gave me the news. It just all made sense and it was good to finally know that all this pain and abnormal spotting was not just in my head. To be honest I don't look at my illness as a negative, I have always looked at it as a lesson and something I obviously need to go through and learn from.

*

SHANDI CLOUSE
Shandi was diagnosed with
endometriosis in 2015 at age 27

I received my endometriosis diagnosis at age twenty-seven in November 2015, from the gynecologist who did my laparoscopy. To a point I was relieved to finally have a name for the pain that had pretty much taken over my life, but on the other hand I was furious that my body had failed me. I questioned whether my diagnosis of irritable bowel syndrome at age fourteen was wrong since the symptoms were identical. The question that weighed the heaviest on me was if the endometriosis was to blame for my miscarriage. The heavy bleeding mimicked what I was experiencing now, and at the time they had thought I had large tumors in my uterus that were never addressed after that emergency room visit. It was all just too much at first.

My gynecologist was very kind in how he went about telling me, and answered every question I had, but fear still took over. As I left his office, knowing this was just the beginning, I had the worst panic attack. The depression hit soon after. Every day I spent hours crying and isolating myself from my family because I felt so guilty about not being able to do everything I used to. More often than not, I felt like a failure as a wife and a mother. It took several months, tons of support, and a lot of self-discovery to get to where I am now. Every day I wake up and remind myself that I can do this, that I can fight this, and that I'm just as much of a woman as I was before my diagnosis. I try to focus more on the present, and on being present in the moment because I know all too well it can change in an instant.

*

PATRICIA CONNELLY
Patricia was diagnosed with
endometriosis in 2014 at age 33

I went to thirteen or so doctors. I was ready to hear "There's nothing wrong with you," again but my last doctor finally did a full female checkup. She sat down and asked me about my pains. Then she said, "It sounds like you have endometriosis. Go to this other doctor." I was somewhat happy because at least I was being heard. The other doctor said, "No, you don't have endometriosis. Here, take these pills." That didn't help. A year later, I was scheduled for a total hysterectomy on December 31, 2014. I had almost stage two endometriosis.

*

SHAUNA COX
Shauna was diagnosed with
endometriosis in 2012 at age 29

At age twenty-nine, after twenty years of suffering from painful periods and now living with pain on other days of my cycle as well, I was finally given an official diagnosis. It had been a long road to get to this point because of faulty belief systems that doctors still carry today. In my case, for example, I was given an ultrasound but when nothing was found, I was written off as not having endometriosis. However, an ultrasound usually doesn't reveal endometriosis. A laparoscopy is needed for diagnosis, and doctors often won't consider that until a woman is struggling to conceive.

My first laparoscopy for suspected endometriosis occurred in March 2012. My husband and I had been trying to get pregnant for eighteen months with no success. Because I had symptoms of endometriosis, my fertility doctor decided to operate to see if he could confirm the diagnosis and discover the reason why we weren't having success in the baby-making department. The surgery went well but upon waking up, the doctor told me, "You're a mess inside, and I don't know why." Adhesions were causing my bowel to be glued to my uterus, my left fallopian tube was removed, and my right ovary was also stuck to the bowel. My left pelvic sidewall and cul-de-sac were also "obliterated due to scarring," according to an operative report.

About five months later, rather than being in pain only on my period, I started to experience severe pelvic pain that was worse when

I wasn't on my period! Every night, I woke in excruciating pain and was up for hours before Tylenol #3 kicked in enough that I could sleep. The pain dulled down enough during the day that I could get through work, but I was exhausted from lack of sleep and constantly dealing with pain. I contacted my fertility doctor again to find out if I might have a cyst, and he agreed to do another laparoscopy to investigate.

This second laparoscopy occurred in November 2012. In this second surgery, I was found to have extensive endometriosis. Finally! Confirmation of a disease that I knew deep down I had, and the hope that now something could finally be done about it! The doctor treated the endometriosis with ablation, which I later learned isn't an effective treatment and can even make matters worse. This surgery helped for about two weeks before the pain returned to the same level of severity it was before. On the plus side, I did finally have a confirmed diagnosis!

I felt relieved on some level to finally have an answer as to why I was experiencing pain and why I wasn't getting pregnant. I felt some hope that maybe there was something we could do now! After researching the disease, a lot of that hope faded away, as I discovered many other women like myself with endometriosis never succeed in getting pregnant. Sure, it wasn't a definite thing and there are lots of women who can conceive. But because we were struggling, and because I had a diagnosis that often did cause infertility, I immediately jumped on the glass half empty wagon and started bracing for a childless life.

*

JORDANNE GOLD
Jordanne was diagnosed with
endometriosis in 2014 at age 22

I was diagnosed by an OB/GYN at the age of twenty-two, but the diagnosis came with no information about the condition. It wasn't until I was home researching the condition when I realized what this diagnosis meant. For the first few months I felt an uncontrollable sadness as I tried to accept the diagnosis. I went through many stages of grief until I truly accepted what was happening to me. Most days, I am emotionally able to handle how life has changed over my journey, however there are days when the anger and sadness creep back into my head.

*

CHRISTA HALL
Christa was diagnosed with
endometriosis in 2015 at age 24

My diagnosis was kind of complicated. I had my first surgery in September 2009, and though no endometriosis was found, severe scar tissue from severe inflammation was found. We now believe that the roots of the endometriosis were there but hadn't yet fully come through. My pain came back even more severe when I went off birth control in 2012, when my husband and I started trying to conceive. I was living in a different state, and couldn't find a gynecologist who would believe me. When I explained my symptoms, I was told either that I couldn't handle the pain that periods brought on, or that I was looking to get attention. My symptoms became so severe that I was in the emergency department almost monthly with pain that made me vomit and pass out. After a few months, they told me I was just looking for narcotics, and red flagged my information.

About two months later, I met Dr. Morowski, a gynecologist who worked in the emergency department. He actually listened to me. He listened about my pain, and explained that I had all the symptoms of endometriosis, which made me feel like I wasn't crazy.

I was on Lupron for four months. After family health issues, we moved in 2014, and I lost my insurance but got it back in 2015. I found a doctor who did the diagnostic laparoscopy and confirmed a diagnosis of endometriosis. I was twenty-four years old. I was actually happy to finally have a diagnosis, to know I wasn't crazy or a hypochondriac like most doctors thought. But over the following months I became very depressed and scared. Realizing I had a chronic pain disease at age twenty-four was intimidating, and the fact that it's lifelong was absolutely terrifying. I'm now resolved with my diagnosis, and try to do the best I can to help women who're having a hard time coming to terms with a chronic pain disease.

*

BETH JENSEN
Beth was diagnosed with
endometriosis in 2009 at age 20

When I was seventeen, in the summer between grades eleven and twelve, I ended up moving out of my mother's home. I came to this major decision as a teenager because I was tired of fighting all the time and not being believed by my own mother. That year I found a doctor who said my pain wasn't normal and I needed to see a gynecologist who specialized in pelvic pain. After getting a referral and seeing my first gynecologist, he suspected I had endometriosis, but the only way to confirm was with diagnostic surgery. I underwent diagnostic surgery in 2009, just as I was turning twenty. What started as a diagnostic laparoscopy turned into ablation of endometriosis. The gynecologist found what he thought was endometriosis and decided to go ahead with removal. During my postop visit, it was explained why I should have taken more time off work, because the surgery ended up not being simple, and pathology indeed confirmed endometriosis.

The gynecologist told me I needed Lupron, a hormone therapy, so the surgery would "stick." I listened to this gynecologist with absolutely no research or second thought about it—because this person went to medical school and had studied for years. This person was supposed to have my best interests at heart, and should know how to fix me. Isn't that what we are taught as children? This is honestly one of my biggest life regrets. Doctors are not magical know-it-all beings, and if they act that way, run far in the other direction.

*

JESSICA NOEL
Jessica was diagnosed with
endometriosis in 1991 at age 9

I started having severe abdominal pain at age seven and went from doctor to doctor for two years, being told it was gas, food allergy, or I was constipated and needed to eat more fiber. During those two years I was put in the psych ward against my mom's permission because doctors thought my symptoms were all in my head.

In September 1990, I met my hero, Dr. Heidi. An endometriosis specialist, she was the first doctor to believe something was wrong. She first ran a bunch of tests and tried treating it with medicine, but when that didn't work, she scheduled exploratory surgery.

On January 20, 1991, I had surgery to determine whether I had endometriosis. When Dr. Heidi came into my room to tell me and my family that I did, in fact, have endometriosis, I felt happy, sad, angry, frustrated, and betrayed. I was happy because I finally had an answer for what was wrong with me. I was sad, angry, frustrated, and betrayed because for two years my mom and I were put through hell, being told I was just making it up. My emotions change from year to year, but one emotion has stayed the same: frustration, because there is no cure and on a daily basis millions of women suffer just to function properly.

*

CARMELA POLLOCK
Carmela was diagnosed with
endometriosis in 1995 at age 25

Prior to the diagnosis, I visited many doctors. One suggested it was in my head and referred me to a psychologist, but my intuition was telling me otherwise. Most months I experienced heavy bleeding and was confined to my bedroom for up to two days. General over-the-counter pain killers helped temporarily, but this was only short lived. I needed someone to listen to me and believe what I was saying.

It was the summer of 1995, and I was twenty-five years old. The endometriosis pain had been consistent each month, until one day I was unable to walk. I woke in the middle of the night struggling to move. I was alone as my partner at that time was away on business. So with no support, I stumbled out of bed to the medical cabinet and took the strongest pain killers I could find. I didn't move after taking those pills. I laid on the floor praying for the pain to dissipate. However, no relief was in sight. After an hour on the cold floor, I knew I had to get help. Again I heaved my body to the closest phone and called for an ambulance. It arrived within ten minutes.

For the next eighteen hours I underwent a battery of blood tests, x-rays, and an ultrasound. The female emergency doctor on duty listened and showed genuine concern. For the first time, I witnessed a medical practitioner who demonstrated compassion and empathy for my pain. She noted that my symptoms were likely associated with endometriosis and referred me to a local gynecologist. She spoke of her own journey with it, and acknowledged the debilitating nature of the disease. I was relieved to know I wasn't a hypochondriac after all, and that someone in the medical field understood.

Five days after being discharged from emergency, I was back in the hospital for laparoscopic surgery. The diagnosis was stage four endometriosis and a ruptured cyst on the left ovary. I will be forever grateful to that emergency doctor who respected the brokenness of my emotions and held me up with compassion and understanding.

*

ASHLEY ROMANKO
Ashley was diagnosed with
endometriosis in 2005 at age 21

I started feeling symptoms in my late teens. After numerous doctor visits, I was finally sent to a gynecologist. I went to see him, told him my symptoms and he said, "You may have endometriosis." I had no idea what that was, but felt a huge weight lifted from my shoulders because I had a diagnosis and someone believed me. I had no idea what this meant. I had no idea it was a life sentence, and there was no cure. I had no idea I would have this pain for the rest of my life, with no break.

*

SAYDA WYMER
Sayda was diagnosed with
endometriosis in 2010 at age 35

I was diagnosed in 2010 when I went to see my primary care provider for severe bleeding and chunks of tissue coming out of my vagina that looked almost like skin. I also had pain during intercourse, which was putting a strain on my marriage. My doctor referred me to an OB/GYN. That doctor said I could very well have endometriosis, but the only way to know for sure was to do a laparoscopic surgery. So we did just that, and the result was positive: I had endometriosis. She cleaned up a lot of adhesions and took out a chocolate cyst which had spilled over, but she was able to save my ovaries, so I was glad for that. I was comfortable for a couple of years before I started having the symptoms again. I didn't fully understand what endometriosis was, and it wasn't until I started feeling pain again that it finally hit me.

*

JACQUIE YOUNG
Jacquelyn was diagnosed with
endometriosis in 2012 at age 22

The diagnosis came when I was twenty-two years old. My pelvic pain was on the right side so my doctor suspected appendicitis, but all the tests were negative. I started my own research, and it became very clear that all my symptoms were consistent with those of a patient with endometriosis. I went to see my gynecologist who said I was too young to have the disease. I begged for a diagnostic laparoscopy, as I was desperate for answers and relief.

After a few months of trying birth control, the gynecologist obliged to doing surgery. It was confirmed that not only did I have endometriosis, but a very severe case—stage four.

I felt so relieved and had validation that I wasn't crazy. Over time, my emotions have remained fairly the same, but I also feel very grateful to have been diagnosed fairly young. Early diagnosis allowed me to preserve my fertility.

*

JENNIFER YOUNG
Jennifer was diagnosed with
endometriosis in 2009 at age 21

I was getting ready to turn twenty-two when I was diagnosed. Both my gynecologist and my family doctor suspected endometriosis since I was sixteen, but a specialist did my surgery and he was the one who found it. I was relieved that I finally had a diagnosis as to why I went through what I did each month (all I knew was my friends didn't go through what I did). I knew there had to be more than just having heavy periods. But I was also crushed when I learned I would probably never be able to have kids, and that I had to live with this disease for the rest of my life.

My emotions have changed since then. I was thrilled when I had two successful pregnancies, but crushed by a suspected miscarriage. I'm now hopeful that by having had a hysterectomy, the doctor got all the endometriosis areas like he said he did.

*

CHAPTER FOUR

Identifying Our Triggers

Your genetics load the gun. Your lifestyle pulls the trigger. -DR. MEHMET OZ

Although the exact cause of endometriosis remains unknown, there are a plethora of triggers unique to each woman. For some, it's certain foods. For others, it's physical activity. But before we can manage the triggers, we must first discover what they are. What triggers have you correlated to a flare of symptoms?

*

ADRIEANNE BEASLEY
Adrieanne was diagnosed with
endometriosis in 2014 at age 31

There are a few different triggers that flare my symptoms: doing heavy or frequent lower body exercises, stress, alcohol, caffeine, meat and dairy. I've changed my diet and eliminated foods that trigger flares, which I do find helps quite a bit. I also try to limit heavy lifting squats or lower body exercises so as not to aggravate my symptoms.

*

SHILOH BRITT
Shiloh was diagnosed with
endometriosis in 2011 at age 22

For me, they were just flare ups. The bane of my endometriosis. There were days when Aleve just wouldn't cut it, I cried as I held my abdomen and slunk to the floor. Flares came on quickly, and lasted for hours. As the disease progressed, so too did the flares. They became more intense and lasted longer, sometimes over a week.

With the flares there was no management, only surviving. This sounds a bit drastic, but when you are consumed with pain and cannot feel outside of it, there is no living; you exist, but do not live. During these times I took narcotics, Vicodin mostly, and as soon as one wore off it was on to the next dose. Heating pads helped on occasion, but it may have just been my delusional mind willing it so. During the beginning and end of the flares, I used a heating pad as well as a type of warming cream, but in the heat of the flare nothing helped except the hardcore pain killers. With each flare, I begged my husband to take me to the emergency room, and for the first three (pre-diagnosis), he did. In the span of two years, I was in the emergency room seven times. Even with insurance, I will be paying these off for years.

*

EMMA CLIFTON
Emma was diagnosed with
endometriosis in 2015 at age 30

My symptoms are my body's way of communicating with me, as there are patterns with my pain and symptoms. Flares happen when

I'm not concentrating on my diet or I'm stressed. I was at my worst when I wasn't honoring myself or my values, when I was miles off my path. Now, whenever I feel a flare up, I always stop and ask myself, how do I feel? If the answer is stressed, I need to look at why. If the answer is exhausted and sluggish, then I need to look at my diet and exercise regime. I practice daily yoga, but also need to move my body and get out in nature once a day. This gets the blood and energy flowing through my body, and helps to calm the mind.

Quite often when we are in a lot of pain, we think about that pain constantly, which can create a swirl of negative thought patterns. The more we focus on it, the worse it gets. Whenever I am in pain, I always try to breathe and focus on an area of my body that isn't in pain. You would be amazed how much the brain can have an impact on our pain management.

*

SHANDI CLOUSE
Shandi was diagnosed with
endometriosis in 2015 at age 27

It took a year to figure out what my triggers were, and it definitely wasn't easy. I had to really pay attention to what I was doing in my daily life: what I was eating, how much I was resting, and to listen to my body when a flare up happened. I ended up taking some advice from a good friend who was also an endometriosis sister about starting the endometriosis diet, which was one of the better choices I made in self-management. It consists of a list of foods that may trigger the worsening of symptoms. Week by week I went down this list one food at a time. I found that my biggest food triggers are red meat, dairy, soy, and too much caffeine, and I had to cut them out completely. Because I have interstitial cystitis, my diet is even more strict, so I switched to a non-processed food diet and made a binder full of safe recipes to keep on hand in the kitchen. Fish is the base protein in nearly all my meals. I switched to eating only fresh vegetables and goat's milk, and even changed from regular iodized salt to pink Himalayan salt. When I grocery shop, I make sure to check the labels on everything I buy to avoid these trigger foods, and I also keep a list of safe brands on hand.

Stress is also a huge trigger for me so I integrated meditation, hula hooping, and light yoga into my daily routine, and I try to rest as often as I can to offset the extreme fatigue. Drinking certain teas, such as chamomile with honey, help with the nausea, and I keep saltine crackers and a water bottle on the nightstand with my heating pad just in case. Now when a flare hits, I ask myself base questions to determine what could have triggered it. Am I overly stressed or not sleeping properly? If so, I know I need to meditate and step back a bit from what's bothering me, and either take frequent naps or go to bed earlier. Have I eaten something recently that I shouldn't have? If that answer is yes, then I need to reevaluate my food intake and cut out whatever is causing the pain to be worse. It's a lot of work some days, but in doing these things over this year, I have managed to greatly reduce the amount of flare ups I go through, and experiencing even just a fraction less of pain makes it worth it.

*

PATRICIA CONNELLY
Patricia was diagnosed with
endometriosis in 2014 at age 33

Walking too much, stressing, dairy products, meat, getting angry, carrying heavy stuff. I keep saying I'm going to regret drinking this milk later, but I'm not going to let endometriosis say I need to stop drinking milk.

*

SHAUNA COX
Shauna was diagnosed with
endometriosis in 2012 at age 29

There are a few triggers that reliably indicate that I'll experience the pain of endometriosis. One is my period. Unfortunately, my period isn't regular enough that I can start medicating ahead of time to try to circumvent the pain. Generally, that means that I either feel like I'm getting my period and so I start taking medication thinking I'm finally going to get ahead of the damn thing and then don't get it, or that means that I wait too long and am in too much pain for the medication to do much.

A second trigger, which isn't quite as reliable, is having a bowel movement. On my period, this usually comes with some pretty intense rectal pain made worse by the Tylenol #3, which causes constipation. When I'm not on my period, it usually involves a dull cramping sensation in my lower pelvis for an hour or so after having a bowel movement. It doesn't happen often enough, however, that I end up fearing a trip to the toilet, so there's an upside to that, I guess!

Perhaps because of the adhesions present in my body that are causing several organs to be fused together, certain movements can also trigger pain: sneezing or coughing when lying down, stretching (although at other times this actually helps the pain), and running. If I can feel a sneeze or cough coming when I'm lying down, I'll often hold my stomach to ease some of the pain that is inevitably to follow. When exercising, there are times where I've had to stop running and walk, or even lie down and brace my tummy until the pain stops. Luckily, like with bowel movements, pain doesn't happen all the time with exercising, so I am still able to work out and keep a relative amount of fitness up in my life.

*

JORDANNE GOLD
Jordanne was diagnosed with
endometriosis in 2014 at age 22

The triggers that I have found that correlate to a flare up have been caffeine, alcohol, and sex. These triggers have always affected me right from the start, and to this day can still affect me. To control these risk factors at my worst I would try to eliminate them completely. Since managing my endometriosis through excision surgery, I have been able to reintroduce these things back into my life.

*

CHRISTA HALL
Christa was diagnosed with
endometriosis in 2015 at age 24

Other than my period and ovulation, I have a few things that trigger a flare, stress being the hardest of all. Because of the damage the scar tissue has done to my intestines, I've found that eating too much gluten or greasy food triggers a flare as well. The best way for me to manage triggers is to try to stay as stress-free as possible, stay out of stressful situations, and do yoga to help calm down if I am feeling more stressed than usual.

My diet is now a ninety percent gluten-free organic diet, and I'm working up to completely gluten-free. Stress has always caused issues for me since I was younger, and by the time I was in high school and experiencing complications, my stomach would swell up to the point that I would look six months pregnant. My gluten intolerance has also gotten progressively worse over the years. When I was a teenager, I would feel a little sick after eating food with gluten, but the worsening symptoms after Lupron included my gluten intolerance making me cramp more than before.

*

BETH JENSEN
Beth was diagnosed with
endometriosis in 2009 at age 20

I have most certainly figured out quite a few of my triggers: intercourse, masturbation, orgasm, alcohol, eating large portions of red meat with no sides, soy products, long walks, not enough sleep, jeans or slacks with little give, lifting or carrying over fifteen pounds, showers which is a major annoyance, coffee (though surprisingly not black tea), and of course cleaning the house for more than about twenty minutes. Most of the triggers are difficult to cut from my life, so for the daily things I have to do, I make sure I stay medicated and try not to push myself too much. Everything else I do in moderation or downright avoid. I rarely go on walks anymore, and trying to get enough sleep while living in chronic pain and being the mother of a toddler is honestly laughable.

*

JESSICA NOEL
Jessica was diagnosed with
endometriosis in 1991 at age 9

I have only three triggers, and try to avoid them at all costs: red meat, overworking my body, and severe cold. I can eat only free-range grass-fed red meat. If I eat any other red meat, I am either in bed for the next three days or in the hospital for pain. If I overwork my body, I am in bed for four days with my heating pad and heated blanket until the flare calms down. Severe cold is hard to avoid since I live in the Northeast, but I do my best to dress in layers. Some days I wear a hot water bottle tied to my waist to combat the cold so my body does not go into a flare. My triggers haven't changed, but I do have less flares since I figured them out.

*

CARMELA POLLOCK
Carmela was diagnosed with
endometriosis in 1995 at age 25

The first nine years after diagnosis, I didn't see a correlation to anything specific that would cause my symptoms to flare. Each month pretty much presented the same—pain plus painkillers equaled bed. It wasn't until my baby arrived that the symptoms changed.

92

I was in my mid-thirties and stress became my bedfellow. Long months of fatigue and new mum stress created an environment in my body that exacerbated the endometriosis, encouraged it to spread, and brought me to my knees month after month. The difference now was that pain and discomfort began about ten days before the actual bleeding started. I could somewhat manage the pain with painkillers, but the frustrating part was the relentless nature of my suffering. I had only a small window of reprieve between one cycle finishing and the next one starting. I again turned to doctors and specialists to manage the pain and symptoms. However, I found this was not enough.

Due to the years of discomfort, I began to live with the perpetual dread of experiencing another month of pain. I felt I wasn't in control of my life and knew very well that I had to manage stress to get relief. To repair the endometriosis bumps and gouges in my body, I turned to journaling and poured out my emotions. Journaling was my solace and salvation. It listened without judgment as I wrote about my pain, stress, and life changes. I later combined this with meditation and felt some relief each month. Over time, the anticipated fear before a cycle dissipated. Through journaling, I acknowledged my courage and the need to heal my body. Endometriosis and the many misdiagnoses had wounded me both physically and emotionally. It was time to take down my defenses and directly address my fears privately. I could see that endometriosis was serving a purpose. I needed to stop fighting and begin showing compassion to my body and learn from the experiences that brought me to this place of pain.

*

ASHLEY ROMANKO
Ashley was diagnosed with
endometriosis in 2005 at age 21

I don't always know when a flare is coming; sometimes there are signs that tell me more pain is coming. It's sort of like my whole body starts heating up and I feel like I'm going to explode because of the pain. If I'm out, then I need to get home quickly. It feels like my whole body stops and then acid is being poured from the inside out of my pelvis. The exhaustion hits me hard and I feel like I'm going to fall down because of the pain. It feels like I'm being cut into pieces and then glued together, and then repeat.

Some of my triggers seem to be stress, overexertion, intercourse, being cold, standing for long periods of time, and sometimes just standing for a short time. All I want is for the pain to stop. I have pain daily and when it worsens, I wish to go back to the day before when the pain wasn't as bad as it is during the flare. It's very hard to be in pain all the time. There's no break. There is a break when you sleep but it's hard to get to sleep because of the pain. And when you awake from sleep, the pain is often worse.

*

SAYDA WYMER
Sayda was diagnosed with
endometriosis in 2010 at age 35

I try to do mild exercises and stretches. I also walk and use a heating pad, but sometimes that doesn't help at all.

*

JACQUIE YOUNG
Jacquelyn was diagnosed with
endometriosis in 2012 at age 22

Some of my triggers are certain foods such as dairy, alcohol and certain carbs. After eating those foods, the pain increases and usually my abdomen swells in size. I try to avoid those trigger foods to help manage my symptoms. Strenuous things such as cleaning, exercise and even sex can cause a flare that can last for days. Over time, the physical activity has gotten much worse for my flare so I try to still be as active as possible, but in little bursts.

The biggest thing is that I've learned my limitations, which is very important. Instead of cleaning my entire house in one day, I'll do sections each day so it's not as overwhelming. One big blessing is that I'm now more in tune with my body.

*

JENNIFER YOUNG
Jennifer was diagnosed with
endometriosis in 2009 at age 21

There was no thing I knew of for certain that would trigger a flare except for these three things: stress, alcohol and sex. When it came to food, I could be fine with something once, the next time would cause a flare, and then next time it would be fine again. The only issues I have now are the random "swelly belly," weight gain, and hot flashes.

There's something about being broken
at various times in your life that makes
you a more complete person.

J. IRON WOOD

*

CHAPTER FIVE

Juggling Treatments

When I'm resting on a flare day, I need to remember that I am not wasting the entire day doing nothing. I am doing exactly what I need to do. I am recovering. -ENDOBODY

Because the exact cause of endometriosis remains unknown, treatment remedies run the gamut and are not an exact science. What works for one woman many not work for another. What medical therapies have been offered? Which have you tried?

*

ADRIEANNE BEASLEY
Adrieanne was diagnosed with
endometriosis in 2014 at age 31

Personally, heat works for my pain and I have a heating pad and a hot water bottle. I also do yoga and meditate which help to relax me. I have changed my diet to be vegan and gluten-free. This helps with some of the flares and some of the abdominal bloating. I take several herbal supplements and vitamins such as omega-3, magnesium, B12, acidophilus, and turmeric. I've also tried acupuncture and found that did give me some pain relief. I was given a prescription for Visanne for four months, however it did not work well for me. The side effects were actually quite horrible, and it didn't reduce any of the pain.

*

SHILOH BRITT
Shiloh was diagnosed with
endometriosis in 2011 at age 22

At first I tried supplements and then physical therapy. I exercised this way, I didn't exercise that way, then meditation. After that, it was light over-the-counter pain medications and then topical creams. I had the birth control pill, then the birth control patch, then a different birth control pill. After that was yet another birth control pill with no days to have a period.

I had acid reflux medicine (because what else could it be?). I tried acupuncture, hypnosis, and the ever popular ignoring of everything. I had a monthly Lupron shot which put me into medical menopause. Finally, I had an IUD.

They all seemed to work for a while (with the exception of the acid reflux meds), some for a few days, and others for a few weeks, but then maybe it was my own mind willing them to work. None worked long. With the failure of each, I felt more confused and betrayed by my body, and sunk into a deeper depression.

I made changes to my diet, first trying a low FOD diet (low fermentable, oligosaccharides, and disaccharides), then gluten-free, followed by dairy-free. After that, we tried cutting meat and I cut caffeine. We later discovered caffeine was one of the only things to help during a flare. It was suggested that I try marijuana, which I declined, arguing that I needed all the brain functions that I had, without any impairment of cognitive abilities. Still, the suggestion was tempting when nothing else had worked.

Then there were the procedures: there was a colonoscopy, pelvic laparoscopy, spinal block and finally, a total hysterectomy. After that, there was nothing left to do.

*

EMMA CLIFTON

Emma was diagnosed with
endometriosis in 2015 at age 30

Once I had my laparoscopy to remove the cyst, they also removed the endometriosis, which I was unaware that I had until I came out of surgery. Upon meeting with my gynecologist after the procedure, she told me that the best thing I could do was get the IUD, and that this would stop my periods and in turn stop the majority of my symptoms and reduce the chance of them coming back.

I decided against this, as I don't believe it to be normal to stop the periods and I did not feel comfortable getting the IUD after hearing many stories.

*

SHANDI CLOUSE
Shandi was diagnosed with
endometriosis in 2015 at age 27

After my diagnosis, I was offered two options: try Lupron injections or have a partial hysterectomy due to the endometrial cells being inside the muscle wall of my uterus. As a teenager, I had watched my mother go through hell while taking the Lupron injections and already knew some of the long-term effects it could have. I was given a week to decide, so I threw myself into doing extensive research on the drug and talked to other people in my support groups about their experiences with it. Ultimately, it was talking to my good friend Rachel about what Lupron had done to her, and how some of the effects were still present five years later. That made it clear that Lupron wasn't for me. I called my doctor that same day and scheduled the partial hysterectomy. Since then, I still have been presented only with the two options of trying Lupron injections, despite bringing up my issues surrounding it, or having surgery to have my ovaries removed, which my doctor will not do until we get the problems with my interstitial cystitis better managed.

*

SHAUNA COX
Shauna was diagnosed with
endometriosis in 2012 at age 29

With my very first period came pain. I was age nine and perhaps because I was so young, nothing was offered to me in terms of pain control. Every month when I got my period, I went home sick from school. I would then lay in bed moaning, crying, and vomiting from the pain. My periods were also very heavy. I don't know how many pairs of panties I destroyed bleeding through pads, and how many sheets on my bed I went through!

When I turned fourteen, my mom brought me to a new doctor to see if there was anything she could offer to help me cope with the pain. That doctor mentioned the possibility of endometriosis and put me on a birth control pill called Marvelon. While the pain was better, I was still coming home sick every month, vomiting from the cramps, and bleeding fairly heavily.

Taking pills was always a struggle for me when I was younger. When I was sixteen, I was in the hospital for almost a month. The nurses literally fought with me to take pills. It wasn't that I didn't want to, my body just seemed incapable of cooperating. I would gag, choke, and end up essentially throwing up any pills they tried to give me. What other sixteen-year-old has had nurses attempt mixing a pill into everything from pudding to applesauce to jam? At least Marvelon was a tiny little pill. But the idea of taking Advil or Tylenol for pain never occurred to me, because swallowing a pill was just too hard.

In my twenties, I finally got over what had probably been a pill phobia. It was then when I started taking Advil to cope with the period pain. It definitely helped, but like with the Marvelon, the pain was never completely gone. I was still missing university, and later college classes, and then work at least once, sometimes twice a month.

When my husband and I started trying to conceive in August 2010, I went off Marvelon and was left with just Advil to get me through the tough days. For some weird reason, my periods actually improved for a little while. It was at this time when I was also offered a real treatment for endometriosis: surgery.

Unfortunately, I hadn't done enough of my own research into the disease, and didn't realize that the only effective treatment is excision surgery. As such, I didn't know any better, and my fertility doctor attempted to get rid of the endometriosis during a second surgery through ablation. I now know this can make endometriosis worse by increasing the inflammation already present in the body. Within a few weeks, the pain was at a ten more days than not. I started having to rely on daily Advil and a long-term prescription of Tylenol #3 to decrease the pain and to help me sleep through the worst bouts in the middle of the night! Clearly the two non-excision surgeries I had were not effective!

Early in 2013, I saw an endometriosis specialist who does excision surgery in my province. She encouraged my husband and me to do whatever it took to get pregnant before opting for surgery. We went through two failed IVF cycles, but have since learned that having excision surgery to get rid of endometriosis increases the odds of pregnancy even without fertility treatments. I am finally seeing a light at the end of the treatment tunnel with the hopes of having effective surgery by a doctor in Toronto, and if he can't help me, then at the Center for Endometriosis Care in Atlanta.

It's sad that it's been such a long road to find doctors who truly know what they're doing with this disease, but I'm also hopeful that there exists at least a few doctors who can take away my pain and also potentially increase my fertility, and give my husband and me our dream of finally having children.

*

JORDANNE GOLD
Jordanne was diagnosed with
endometriosis in 2014 at age 22

Throughout my journey I have tried many different medical therapies including birth control pills, excision surgery, pain killers, and the Mirena IUD. The pain management I used over the years includes Toradol, Tramacet, Percocet, Voltaren suppositories, and morphine, all of which helped control my pain levels. The only medical treatment that has truly helped has been excision surgery, which was performed by an endometriosis specialist.

*

CHRISTA HALL
Christa was diagnosed with
endometriosis in 2015 at age 24

I have only done two medical therapies since starting my journey with endometriosis. Before my diagnosis, I was put on a constant birth control pill and skipped my period every month for two years straight. While on birth control, I didn't have any pain aside from that experienced during my period. Before the two years had passed, I started listening to my body more to see what I needed, and knew that going without a period for so long wasn't normal. I switched to a new gynecologist who immediately took me off the pill. He observed me month to month, checking in to see how I was feeling, and if the pain had come back. It had, which prompted my first surgery.

After my surgery, we felt it best to restart my birth control, but to have a period only every three months. I stopped my birth control in 2012 to try to get pregnant, and restarted in 2015 to do testing with our fertility clinic. Being on the birth control has definitely helped my overall pain when I am on it. While I cramp during ovulation, and while I am on my period, it's not as severe.

On top of the birth control pills, I also tried monthly injections of a drug called Lupron, which suppresses the signals from the pituitary glands to induce menopause. I was twenty-two years old when I was on this medication. It was very hard for me to adjust to life as a "menopausal" woman in her twenties, which most people didn't understand how that was happening.

Though the Lupron did help with my symptoms, I had to stop the injections after four months because the side effects were too severe. When I stopped the injections and it was out of my system completely (which took about three months before I even started having a period again) my pain came back worse than it had ever been. I was in near constant pain, and the severity changed from day to day, depending on my stress levels and where I was at in my cycle.

*

BETH JENSEN
Beth was diagnosed with
endometriosis in 2009 at age 20

This question requires a lot of thinking on my part, trying to remember all the small attempts among the large ones is proving to be difficult. Over the years, I was offered different hormonal therapies such as birth control, which I started at age twelve. The big problem with this is that eventually they stopped helping with the pain, and my periods became erratic as I was on continuous birth control.

The last birth control I used before my hysterectomy was the Mirena IUD. I tried it twice and it didn't help due to my tiny uterus that was black and diseased. After surgery in 2009, I also used a so-called hormone therapy called Trelstar which induced chemical menopause-like symptoms. I found out years later that Trelstar is just a brand of Lupron, which helped explain why a bunch of temporary side effects didn't stay temporary.

I've been left with lifelong side effects because I didn't do my research, I just simply believed my doctor because I was young and naïve. I've also been offered surgeries, and have had three, one with a gynecologist who ended up doing more damage than help, and the other two by excision specialists. The two done by the specialists seem to have helped a little by cutting my daily pain level from an eight to about a six. I have also been offered pain medication to help when things like birth control failed to provide relief. Due to my allergy to all types of NSAIDs, I was given the opioid option.

*

JESSICA NOEL
Jessica was diagnosed with
endometriosis in 1991 at age 9

I've been offered all there is for people with endometriosis. I tried several medications, and the only one that gave me some relief was Lupron. But when I discontinued it, my symptoms returned tenfold.

*

CARMELA POLLOCK
Carmela was diagnosed with
endometriosis in 1995 at age 25

With the diagnosis of endometriosis and subsequent laparoscopy surgery, my gynecologist provided a menu of pain management options. He confirmed at this point that there was no guarantee the endometriosis wouldn't return along with painful periods. Ponstan and Nurofen were my friends for many years. I generally didn't leave home without one or two in my handbag, just in case. My gynecologist also suggested a combination contraceptive pill to control pain and reduce menstrual bleeding. Unfortunately, this option was short lived. I experienced daily nausea, fatigue and low blood pressure which would drop without warning, making it too dangerous to drive.

Later, with the birth of my son, I became increasingly ill. Over-the-counter and prescription medications weren't working as well as they had previously. The long days of abdominal and back pain, fatigue and general unwellness left me despondent, angry and frustrated. The endometriosis had spread, fibroids were growing, and I suffered a miscarriage.

After more surgery failed to provide any long-term results, my gynecologist gently raised the idea of a hysterectomy, knowing that my husband and I would welcome a second child. She concluded that the level of pain coupled with frequent heavy bleeds required a more determined surgical approach. I respected her recommendation as she was well versed on the debilitating effects endometriosis had on my physical, mental and emotional state. Her advice was further supported by the frequent growth of fibroids that plagued my uterus, including adenomyosis (thickening of the uterus), since the birth of my son.

The road leading to a hysterectomy decision was a difficult one. I wanted freedom from the chronic pain. My son needed his mum back, my husband his wife, and myself—a vibrant and happy me without pain and suffering. Surprisingly though, I found myself grieving for the child we would not have and the loss of the one organ that could make this happen. In the four weeks leading up to the surgery I connected to my heart, acknowledging and understanding the future loss of the womb I still had. I turned to friends and family for comfort, but the road not traveled was not easily understood.

I entered surgery with a positive mind and heart. Accepting the hysterectomy was the right decision. I knew there would be no healing without courage, so I walked myself in, refusing the trolley bed. I stood tall in the understanding that it was going to be okay and life would change for the better. And, indeed, my decision was the right one. To this day I have no pain and life is simply amazing.

*

ASHLEY ROMANKO
Ashley was diagnosed with
endometriosis in 2005 at age 21

I've been offered all sorts of medical therapies and have tried continuous birth control, Visanne, a chiropractor, physiotherapy, topical pain gel, pain clinic, pain medication, and anti-inflammatory medication. I will continue to try therapies to find out what will work for me. What works for one, may not work for another and what doesn't work for someone, may work for someone else. No one case is the same as another.

*

SAYDA WYMER
Sayda was diagnosed with
endometriosis in 2010 at age 35

I was first offered pelvic floor therapy, but I didn't like it so I didn't finish that treatment. I felt it wasn't helping anyway. Then the doctor recommended I go through with laparoscopic surgery and the Mirena for treatment. So far that is the treatment that I continue to have.

*

JACQUIE YOUNG
Jacquelyn was diagnosed with
endometriosis in 2012 at age 22

Throughout the years of dealing with endometriosis, I have been offered many medical therapies. Excision surgery brought the most relief out of all the treatments. Before seeing a specialist, other doctors simply burned the disease, making it more painful.

Another treatment that has helped tremendously has been the Mirena IUD. It helps control the adenomyosis (internal endometriosis within the uterus). It allows me to not have to suffer through periods because I no longer get them. Pelvic floor physical therapy has also helped manage my symptoms. It does take patience, as the results are not linear. Each week comes with challenges, but it's been a year since I've been in physical therapy and it has made such a difference in my pelvic spasms. The worst treatment was a nasal hormone spray called Synarel (basically Lupron), which provided no relief at all.

Birth control was the first option, and it didn't provide relief as I hadn't had a surgery during that time.

*

JENNIFER YOUNG
Jennifer was diagnosed with
endometriosis in 2009 at age 21

My surgery brought relief for a few months, but then the pain returned. With my pregnancies, while it was nice to not have a period those nine months with each, the pain was still there as the scar tissue stretched and tore as my uterus grew. Really, the only thing that would help half the time before my hysterectomy was medicine and a heating pad. I tried all kinds of birth control methods and each worked for a short while and then stopped, so I would have to move on to the next birth control. After a while, they had all stopped working for me.

*

The moment you accept yourself,
you become beautiful.
OSHO

*

CHAPTER SIX

Toolbox of Relief

Being able to walk pain-free is a blessing. Being able to walk without showing the pain is a skill. -KYLIE MCPHERSON

Many endometriosis sufferers find traditional medical therapies aren't enough, and seek alternative and naturopathic remedies to augment her toolbox. Ranging from acupuncture to yoga and meditation to medicinal marijuana, herbal therapies and beyond, what each woman keeps in her armory is whatever brings the most relief. Which remedies and self-management tools help you the most?

*

ADRIEANNE BEASLEY
Adrieanne was diagnosed with
endometriosis in 2014 at age 31

I would highly recommend yoga and heat therapy to anyone else who suffers from endometriosis. I would also recommend that they see a naturopath. I found that acupuncture and heat help with pain. Yoga helps me to relax, which also helps with pain.

*

SHILOH BRITT
Shiloh was diagnosed with
endometriosis in 2011 at age 22

Though nothing completely alleviated my symptoms, there were a few things that lessened them, for a time anyway. I figured these out on my own through trial and error. Caffeine helped me handle the pain, as did Aleve in conjunction with Tiger Balm (a heating cream meant for sore muscles). These two helped me sit though class or get through a work shift, but only seemed to help when pain was below a certain point. When I was at home, I curled up with a heating pad.

On days when nothing seemed to work and the pain was too much for me to function (unable to work or go to school on these days), I would take Vicodin and cry. The only relief I was able to find was in my dreams. It got to the point that all I wanted to do was sleep.

I cried. A lot. During a flare it seemed that all I did was cry, and in some ways that helped me. It might not have been rational, it might not have been appropriate, but it always seemed to help in some way.

For me, one of the best things to do was to talk about what I was going through with my mom. Knowing that she believed me was the most powerful medicine I ever had—then I didn't feel so alone and I had hope that I wouldn't be in pain forever.

*

EMMA CLIFTON
Emma was diagnosed with
endometriosis in 2015 at age 30

My idea behind wanting to manage and hopefully one day beat my endometriosis is through complementary therapies. I teach and practice yoga daily, even if it's just sitting in a child's pose for five minutes. I meditate regularly, and eighty percent of the time I stick to a diet specially designed for endometriosis which consists of avoiding red meat, gluten, caffeine, dairy, soy and limiting alcohol to special occasions or a couple of glasses of wine on the weekend.

I also just started taking BioMedica VegeNAC once a day, which a naturopath recommended. This combination has been fantastic for me since my surgery. I really only get pain during my period, mainly on the first day, and I may have to take pain killers on this day.

I believe diet plays a huge part in endometriosis, as does stress. If these two things can be managed, and you truly listen to your body's feedback like when eating certain foods and noticing when you are stressed, you can then manage the stress in the form of meditation, yoga, float tanks, exercise, art or whatever helps you to relax.

*

SHANDI CLOUSE
Shandi was diagnosed with
endometriosis in 2015 at age 27

Due to the lack of options, I turned to several self-management tools such as altering my diet, meditation, hula hooping, and support groups geared around others suffering from endometriosis. It took nearly a year for the combination to really start working in an effective way for me. I noticed within a few months that the endometriosis diet was reducing my flare ups a few times a month, and that the regular exercise and stress management was helping my mental health as well.

Ultimately, it was being able to connect with other women who were going through the same things that really helped me, and still does. I advocate that anyone suffering from endometriosis find a good support group so they have others to ask questions, trade advice with what they have learned and what works, and to have friends they can rely on when it gets difficult to deal with. Without the small support group I had, I would not have had the strength to overcome the fear or to take care of my illness the way I have. I owe them so much for standing beside me through it all.

Also, knowing your triggers can make a huge difference. Stress was my biggest one. Having an outlet through hula hooping on days when I could move around, and meditation for the days I couldn't, improved my overall mental state which prepared me for what needed to be done, and just dealing with daily life.

*

SHAUNA COX
Shauna was diagnosed with
endometriosis in 2012 at age 29

Both my mom and my great-aunt suggested heat as an alternative therapy to the pain I was experiencing with my period. My great-aunt suffered from pain when she was menstruating, and she told me she found relief sitting on a warm dryer. My mom swore by a hot water bottle. So, growing up, I would get my period, and my mom would warm up our water bottle as hot as she could make it, and as hot as my body could tolerate. Sometimes I'd get her to run a steaming hot bath, and submerge my aching, throbbing belly into it.

The hot water bottle is something I've turned to as an adult, except it's now a microwaveable rice bag with Velcro straps so I can secure it around myself as tightly as I can to my pelvis. The scorching bath is also still a favorite therapy of mine. There are times when even Tylenol #3 won't take the pain away, but a scorching bath will help for as much as thirty minutes, allowing me to rest my muscles for a bit before the pain comes back in full force.

I have also been so desperate from the pain that I have turned to marijuana on a couple occasions. On one occasion, it helped me sleep when all I wanted was to sleep the pain away. On a second occasion, however, it intensified the pain. Ever since then, I've been afraid to try it again, in case it just focuses my attention back on the pain again.

While I have debated trying other tools like anti-inflammatory diets, acupuncture and massage, I'm not sure I fully believe in them and I feel as if not believing would make it that much harder for them to work on me. That being said, I would recommend to anyone with endometriosis to try everything you can within your means until you are able to get effective excision surgery. Find what works for you and keep doing it, whether or not it's a "proven" therapy. If it helps, great!

If not, move on to something else and never lose hope! There will be some strategy, some therapy, some trick that will help the pain and discomfort, even if just for a few minutes. We are all different, and may all require different methods to get through the day.

*

JORDANNE GOLD
Jordanne was diagnosed with
endometriosis in 2014 at age 22

Aside from different medical therapies, I've tried naturopathy, pelvic floor therapy, diet changes, and herbs. Through my naturopath, I was able to create a list of herbs and vitamins to help manage my endometriosis. The herbs and supplements I found helpful were omega-3, vitamin E, turmeric, and evening primrose oil. Pelvic floor therapy was extremely helpful. My physiotherapist was able to create a huge difference in my daily pain, as well as the pain I felt during sex. I changed my diet to reflect vegan, gluten-free, strict eating, although I found that prior to excision surgery my diet had very little effect on the pain. I would recommend to anyone suffering with endometriosis to see a recognized endometriosis specialist along with seeing a pelvic floor therapist and a naturopath.

*

CHRISTA HALL
Christa was diagnosed with
endometriosis in 2015 at age 24

I have a lot of self-management tools that I picked up while being uninsured. My mother is a massage therapist and gives me weekly massages to help with the sciatica I have from inflammation, as well as stomach massages. I also use an essential oil blend called Deep Muscle Relief or Panaway with peppermint oil to help relieve pain. My heating pad has become my best friend over the course of the years, and is the best comforting tool I have during a flare. I also do a yoga segment at least twice weekly called "hip opener," which helps open up the hips and stretch the back, as well as strengthens your core muscles. The combination of all of these are very effective for me, and I always recommend them to anyone that is suffering and needs daily relief without having to use narcotics.

*

BETH JENSEN
Beth was diagnosed with
endometriosis in 2009 at age 20

I've tried changing my diet, which didn't help much. I also use a heating pad to help when the pain is too much to manage. I actually own two now, because having your heating pad die and not having a backup is never fun. I also want to mention that for me personally I ended up turning to marijuana to help with pain and daily living activities. For years I had to hide that I found something that truly helped due to the stigma. I asked countless doctors to please prescribe medicinal marijuana so I could avoid heavy opioids, but for years I was turned down because they were afraid of losing their medical license or simply because they had a moral objection to it. This is the most effective pain management tool I have ever found, it kept me eating and it kept me moving.

My husband has told me that he has watched me bounce between eighty-five and one hundred five pounds for years. Thankfully, I finally found a doctor who was willing to prescribe a marijuana prescription, but he warned me that this meant that if I ever needed something stronger like the opioids again, I wouldn't be allowed to have them prescribed to me. It was literally one option or the other. Since saying yes, I'm now up to one hundred and thirty pounds, and feel and look healthier than I have in years.

*

JESSICA NOEL
Jessica was diagnosed with
endometriosis in 1991 at age 9

After coming off Lupron, I turned to natural herbs and a type of workout called PiYo which has helped greatly. I tell others to take baby steps and try ginger first, whether it be raw or in tea form, to help with the bloating and pain.

*

CARMELA POLLOCK
Carmela was diagnosed with
endometriosis in 1995 at age 25

In the eight years leading up to the final decision to have a hysterectomy, I embraced a number of complementary therapies, all with the sole purpose of putting my health back on a healing trajectory. The many therapists I consulted designed treatment based on balancing the hormonal cycle, cleansing the body and restoring my immune system. I understood from my research that natural therapies may be a long-term process, but this did not discourage me. I wanted to take control of my own treatment and not place all of my eggs into the one western medicine basket. A holistic approach also meant that my emotional and spiritual self could be taken into consideration, as western medicine clearly neglected this in the past. I had decided that I would not mix modalities to ensure I could identify what worked.

Herbal medicine was my first port of call based on the research I had done, and one that had been used extensively by women with endometriosis. The Chinese herbalist dispensed a concoction of raw herbs that I boiled up into a thick muddy consistency twice a day. I endured the foul tasting liquid for over six months. I did see a slight difference in the severity of my bleeds, but the pain was still present. A positive side effect was that it did reduce the fluid retention leading up to menstruation. The longer term strategy with herbs was dispensing premixed herbal drops under the tongue once a day. This was far more palatable and didn't require all the preparation. After twelve months, symptoms remained.

Traditional Chinese medicine (TCM) was the next modality. I had read many success stories about TCM in treating endometriosis and fertility. I felt positive about embarking on a TCM path and couldn't wait to start it, even though I have a fear of needles. I attended fortnightly, then monthly treatments for eight months. TCM did not reduce my pain but it did raise my energy levels to allow me to push through on the difficult days. The practitioner also recommended that I make dietary alterations. This consisted of no gluten, dairy or processed foods with loads of fresh fruit, vegetables and limited amounts of lean meats. For the first month the diet was difficult, as my body went through a cleansing process and the energy levels hit rock bottom. Almost like a switch, my body changed and I generally felt better, but unfortunately the monthly pain remained.

I reluctantly stopped TCM for one reason—the pain did not subside. Endometriosis continued to compromise my abilities to function as a mum, wife and employer.

Following TCM, I turned to chiropractic treatment. Lower back pain was a consistent symptom of my endometriosis experience. I felt the correlation between my lower back pain and chiropractic treatment principle—that all body structures, including organs and blood vessels, have a nerve supply and it is the spinal column where all the body's nerves radiate—was an important one to investigate in relation to my endometriosis pain. For twelve months, I had fortnightly then monthly appointments where the chiropractor stretched and mobilized my joints and gave me a gentle lower back massage. He also suggested some light exercise to maintain improvements and strengthen my lower back.

Like most of the modalities I tried, I experienced improvements in some areas of my health and well-being, but the endometriosis continued to grow and the pain remained persistent. There came a point where I became despondent and angry at my body. I was grateful for the surprising health changes that herbs, TCM, diet and chiropractic treatments and changes afforded me, but an ultrasound had shown I had developed two fibroids located in the uterine cavity and the wall of my uterus. Several months later, I suffered a miscarriage. The news rocked my world.

Following the last scan and miscarriage, I needed to regroup and cease all alternative therapy treatments so I could get my mental health in order. After the many years of pain and other complications, my behavior became super sensitive and reactive. I arrived at my choice point and I chose to mend my emotional self.

Pain had put up a wall and I needed to take down my defenses and stop focusing on my suffering—my physical self. What I craved was a spiritual healing to peel my life like an onion to identify and acknowledge why endometriosis was such a powerful force in my life. I turned to spiritual healers to rescue my emotional self, repair the past, and refocus my attention to what I could control—the present.

Mindfulness practice was my strength. In moments of silence and contemplation, my body and mind were free to rest. I surrendered the fight and made important decisions regarding my health and long-term goals to mend the broken body I struggled to understand.

*

ASHLEY ROMANKO
Ashley was diagnosed with
endometriosis in 2005 at age 21

A couple of the complementary therapies I turned to were meditation and nutrition. I strongly recommend meditation and keeping your mind distracted so you aren't consumed with pain thoughts. If you can do this before the pain has flared, it can help immensely. Trying to get back on track during a bad flare is much harder than trying to prevent the flare. It takes practice and doesn't always work, but it's worth it when it does.

*

SAYDA WYMER
Sayda was diagnosed with
endometriosis in 2010 at age 35

I tried herbal teas in addition to stretches and mild exercises. The Mirena has made a big difference as it has stopped my menstrual cycle completely. Before this I would go months, if not years, with the heavy bleeding. Each time I showered, it was overwhelming and nightmarish to try to hold a maxi pad between my legs while I was drying off, otherwise blood would run down my legs. I felt uncomfortable, and if I sneezed I would have to run to the bathroom and change. Horrible, horrible!! My self-management tools consist of heating pads, stretching exercises, and pelvic floor exercises which consist of kegel exercises and tightening the abdomen. It alleviates the intense cramping and pain, but not for long.

*

JACQUIE YOUNG
Jacquelyn was diagnosed with
endometriosis in 2012 at age 22

I have gone to get massages and to the chiropractor. The most beneficial complementary therapy was the full body massage. I was pain free for two hours after one session, it was truly amazing! I recommend finding your personal zen, even if it's as simple as a hot bath and a nice cup of tea. I also don't want others to feel as if they are alone in this fight. Endometriosis is not only physically painful, but emotionally. It's best to just take one day at a time and allow yourself to feel your true emotions.

*

JENNIFER YOUNG
Jennifer was diagnosed with
endometriosis in 2009 at age 21

I have found that it's extremely hard to recommend something to someone. Every woman is different, and each endometriosis case is different. What works for one person will not always work for another. In fact, ninety-nine percent of the time when I recommend something, it didn't work for that person like it did for me.

*

All of life is peaks and valleys. Don't let the peaks get too high or the valleys too low.
JOHN WOODEN

*

CHAPTER SEVEN

Coping with Side Effects

Courage does not always roar. Sometimes courage is the quiet voice at the end of the day saying "I will try again tomorrow." -MARY ANNE RADMACHER

A side effect is an adverse reaction to a medication or regimen. As we seek relief from endometrial pain, we sometimes discover unintended consequences from the different remedies we hope will bring relief. What side effects, if any, did you experience along your journey?

*

ADRIEANNE BEASLEY
Adrieanne was diagnosed with endometriosis in 2014 at age 31

I had horrible side effects from Visanne including depression, anxiety, hairloss, mood swings, digestive issues, acne, and weight gain. My acne and depression were quite severe. Continuing treatment with Visanne wasn't worth it, and I went off it after four months.

*

SHILOH BRITT
Shiloh was diagnosed with
endometriosis in 2011 at age 22

The worst and most common side effect was nothing. Zero. Zilch. Not a darn thing changing—and losing a little more hope after every new trial. The Lupron shot put me into a medical menopause where I was getting hot flashes for the entire nine months I was on it. Hot. Cold. Hot. Hot. Freezing. It got to the point where my husband told me my thermostat privileges were suspended. At twenty-three, I was not prepared to be in a menopause of any sort.

Many of the medications gave me an upset stomach, but that also may have just been from pain. The harsher medications like Vicodin dampened my mood, made me lethargic and unable to comprehend. More often than not they made me moody and short with people. I was tired of being in pain, and had a difficult time hiding it the longer it progressed. My husband will be quick to add that my sexual appetite was nonexistent. Whether it was from the medication or constant pain, I will never know. In our young marriage we had little intimacy, and this took a toll on us.

*

EMMA CLIFTON
Emma was diagnosed with
endometriosis in 2015 at age 30

No, not as of yet. I had my laparoscopy about nine months ago now, and some of my spotting and pains are starting to come back, but nowhere near what it was like for years prior to the surgery.

*

SHANDI CLOUSE
Shandi was diagnosed with
endometriosis in 2015 at age 27

There have been many side effects from the treatments and management tools I've tried in the last year. When I first shifted my diet after my diagnosis, my body retaliated even though it was a slow transition. I got an upset stomach and the nausea got worse. For a good two months it seemed to aggravate my interstitial cystitis because my system wasn't used to the changes I was making. My anxiety worsened in the weeks leading up to my partial hysterectomy, and I became moody and easily agitated. Following surgery, I was a mess. My hormones were out of whack, my depression deepened, and mentally I hit rock bottom. While hula hooping helped with the depression and was a great form of exercise, doing it too much caused the pain to worsen, and I could only use my heating pad for so long.

Because I was never prescribed any pain medication, I had to be very careful with how much over-the-counter medicine I took along with my prescriptions for arthritis, severe fibromyalgia and secondary Reynaud's syndrome, thoracic outlet syndrome, and a cervical spinal cord injury. The over-the-counter medication hardly did any good, and caused problems with my irritable bowel syndrome. As of now I am still not prescribed any type of pain medication for it. The only self-management tool I didn't experience any bad side effects from was meditation. In fact it has done a world of good for my mental and physical health and has become a key part in my daily routine.

*

SHAUNA COX
Shauna was diagnosed with
endometriosis in 2012 at age 29

I'm not sure whether the increase in symptoms after my second laparoscopy surgery involving laser ablation was as a result of surgery, or as a coincidence and natural progression of the disease. Either way, after the second surgery my pain got worse and stayed at a seven to ten every day and night for several months. It got to the point where I began feeling as if I might never find anyone who could help me. At times I believed I was going to be in pain forever. I felt hopeless and unsure how I was going to cope with this for the rest of my life. Whether or not the laser made things worse, it definitely didn't help my situation at all.

I suppose side effects from pain medication are only natural, especially when taking them as often as I have the last few years. I've been lucky lately in that most days are tolerable without any pain medication. Some days when I'm in pain, all I need are a couple of Advil to get through. When I need to take Tylenol #3 on really bad days, I know that I am taking it with the anticipation of being in pain from the side effects a couple days later.

I find that I tend to get constipated from the Tylenol #3 and, perhaps because I have endometriosis on my bowel, I am in fairly severe pain when constipated and then need even more Tylenol #3. It becomes a vicious cycle. I get to the point sometimes when I am in pain, I take Tylenol #3 and the pain gets better. But then I'm in pain from constipation and take Tylenol #3, the pain gets better, and so on but to the point when I need to just tough it out so the constipation, and pain that goes along with that, will go away. It's an imperfect system, but there are the days when I can't do anything unless I take the medication, and so I do, despite the knowledge that the side effects may come along too.

In the summer of 2015, I also experienced increased pain during my second fresh IVF cycle. Doctors at the fertility clinic explained that it was probably a result of the fertility medications aggravating or stimulating the endometriosis. I had intense pelvic pain along with pain shooting up and down my right thigh for close to the two months that the IVF cycle took. So now I was not only having trouble getting pregnant and having to spend thousands of dollars in an attempt to do so, but I was potentially also making the endometriosis (the reason for not getting pregnant!) worse. Which would potentially mean, in my mind at least, that each additional attempt would be that much harder. Yet another glass half empty thought on the bandwagon.

*

JORDANNE GOLD
Jordanne was diagnosed with
endometriosis in 2014 at age 22

Through my journey of trying different treatments, the majority of side effects came from the birth control pill. I have tried three different brands, all of which caused weight gain, depression, and mood swings which greatly affected my life, taking away who I was as a person. The side effects made it unbearable to be on them.

*

CHRISTA HALL
Christa was diagnosed with
endometriosis in 2015 at age 24

It's been two and a half years since my last Lupron injection.
When I was on them, I had extreme side effects including chronic
migraines, extreme weight gain, chronic fatigue, moodiness, severe
anxiety and depression. I was unable to control the side effects of the
injections, and when my depression got to the point where I was self-
harming, we decided to stop. It takes a few months for your system to
get back on track, and when I was finally regulated, my endometriosis
symptoms were more severe than they were before the injections.

To this day, I still suffer from chronic migraines, chronic fatigue
and mood swings, and it has taken me a long time to lose the weight
that I gained while on the injection. Because of the weight that I gained
(I gained over sixty pounds in a five-month period), I have more self-
esteem problems that have affected my anxiety and depression.

*

BETH JENSEN
Beth was diagnosed with
endometriosis in 2009 at age 20

There have been numerous side effects over the years from the
treatments, some have been temporary and some permanent. I now
have permanent bone loss and my mouth is riddled with cavities, no
matter how good my dental hygiene is. I have hot and cold flashes as
well as pretty bad mood swings, some of which can throw me into a

deep depression. The side effects of the surgeries have left me with permanent nerve damage that causes daily pain. So far the only way I've been able to keep this at bay is with a nerve blocker, but when it gets chilly or cold, I can lose feeling in my fingers and toes.

*

JESSICA NOEL
Jessica was diagnosed with
endometriosis in 1991 at age 9

I could not be on any birth control, it made my endometriosis worse. Coming off Lupron, my cycles were very heavy and my cyst and pain were ten times worse than before I was put on it. After switching to PiYo and natural herbs, I am doing a lot better.

*

CARMELA POLLOCK
Carmela was diagnosed with
endometriosis in 1995 at age 25

I relied on Ponstan and Nurofen to alleviate the pain, but unfortunately the side effect was nausea. I soldiered on, as the abdominal pain was far worse. The other medication was a combo contraceptive pill to control pain and reduce menstruation. Unfortunately, my blood pressure would drop without warning, leaving me faint and dizzy. In consultation with my doctor, I stopped the medication and sought alternative therapies and treatment. In picking an alternative therapist, I neglected to seek recommendations or question therapists accordingly. I guess this came from my frustration to just get my body fixed, as the years felt like an eternity.

With hindsight, look for people who endorse an alternative therapist rather than choosing one from online or paper sources.

I experienced questionable treatment from a number of therapists who were less than professional and failed to listen. Communicating a course of treatment in layman's terms, including possible side effects is important, particularly when you are using both western and alternative treatments. I would also recommend alternative therapists who specialize in and are well versed in the female anatomy and applicable western medicine treatments. A specialist will be able to provide you with a deeper breadth of options specific to your issue rather than a blanket approach.

*

ASHLEY ROMANKO
Ashley was diagnosed with
endometriosis in 2005 at age 21

I was on Visanne for six months and had horrible side effects. I was told to stay on it for six months because the side effects might stop. They didn't. I had hair loss, headaches, sweats, nausea, and my mood was psychotic. It didn't help me with the pain either, but other women have had success with it and some haven't.

*

SAYDA WYMER
Sayda was diagnosed with
endometriosis in 2010 at age 35

The only side effect I've noticed is that my bellybutton is tender to touch and feels different. Sometimes it hurts when I'm showering.

*

JACQUIE YOUNG
Jacquelyn was diagnosed with
endometriosis in 2012 at age 22

The side effects from the nasal spray Snyarel were absolutely horrific. My hair started to fall out in clumps, it flared up my pain to the point that I could barely walk. My joints hurt at the age of twenty-four, and I knew something wasn't right. It also made me very emotional. One minute I was crying, the next I wanted to scream. I felt like I wasn't in control of my body. I couldn't handle it, so after three very long months which felt like an eternity, I stopped taking it.

*

JENNIFER YOUNG
Jennifer was diagnosed with
endometriosis in 2009 at age 21

The only side effects I've had was that I was allergic to one of the birth control medicines from the get-go and one of the pain medications I was prescribed, and broke out in hives. I became addicted to it, and it caused me to be depressed and suicidal without it, and I formed an allergy to it.

*

Being in control of your life and having realistic
expectations about your day-to-day challenges
are the keys to stress management.
MARILU HENNER

*

CHAPTER EIGHT

Impact on Relationships

The worst thing you can do to a person with an invisible illness is make them feel like they need to prove how sick they are. -ENDOBODY

When we suffer from invisible conditions involving chronic pain, it has a ripple effect on other areas of our life including relationships. Some of our relationships are understanding and supportive while others bear the brunt of the disorder. What relationships have been impacted the most by your endometriosis?

*

ADRIEANNE BEASLEY
Adrieanne was diagnosed with
endometriosis in 2014 at age 31

The relationship that has been most affected by my endometriosis would be my relationship with my husband. Our relationship has improved with time, but before I was first diagnosed it was really difficult. Between the unpredictable bleeding or the pain while having sex, it put a lot of strain on our sex life. These issues made me feel like a horrible wife and I felt like this was not what he signed up for.

In the beginning it was really frustrating for him to understand. Since I've joined a support group and he has come out to some of our information nights, he has a better understanding of endometriosis. He's been by my side throughout this difficult journey, and I honestly do not know if I could do it without him.

It has also affected my friendships as well, because I don't always feel up to going out due to pain and flares. To some of my friends it seems like I've always got some sort of excuse as to why I can't go out, therefore I have lost friendships, which is heartbreaking. My really close friends have learned about endometriosis so they can understand why I can't do everything I would like to. This means the world to me.

*

SHILOH BRITT
Shiloh was diagnosed with
endometriosis in 2011 at age 22

I've lost friends who got tired of me cancelling plans due to pain, friends who believed I was just seeking attention, friends who didn't believe in me when I said something was wrong. In retrospect, these were not friends at all, but it still hurt to have them not understand and abandon me when I was most vulnerable.

My condition nearly ended my marriage. My husband has always been supportive, but would get frustrated with the lack of results (and intimacy). For a time, even he questioned my symptoms. We wanted to have children, and not being able to was a blow for our marriage. People urged him to seek a divorce from me, saying I was overly dramatic and would eat through all his income with my medical bills. Still, this man has stuck with me, and has done everything in his power to get me the best care. I will always be grateful.

To this day, he says the hardest thing for him during this whole endometriosis ordeal was his inability to make it better. He felt helpless as his wife cried herself to sleep nightly.

My relationship with my parents and siblings was uncertain for a time; first it became strained, then strengthened. Having all my parents' attention on me was difficult for my younger siblings. After we got the diagnosis, our relationship grew and strengthened. My mom, especially, was at every appointment and was the first person I called when I felt helpless. She empowered me when I felt I had none.

My mother-in-law went from slightly disliking me to outright hating me. I still don't understand why, but I believe my disease has something to do with it.

My best friend, who was living across the country, and I became closer. In the weeks before my hysterectomy, I wrote her every day, sending her giant letters by week's end. She replied to every one and sent me empowering messages more often than I could count.

Ties I had with relatives were strengthened as they became aware of what I was going through. I had more support than I could've ever expected, coming from family I would have never expected it from.

My working relationships became tumultuous. Because of pain, I was unpredictable and therefore not reliable. I couldn't perform all of my job duties much of the time, and was often short with my coworkers and customers. My manager didn't know what to do with me. Sometimes I'm amazed I didn't lose my job over my disease. I can never thank my manager enough for working with me (and my many doctors' notes), and urging me to keep looking for a cure. Then there were the strangers. People who I had never met or was only briefly acquainted with that shared commonality with what I was going through. They offered love and support when I least expected it.

*

SHANDI CLOUSE
Shandi was diagnosed with
endometriosis in 2015 at age 27

Nearly all my relationships were impacted by my endometriosis, but it hit my family the hardest. It was a huge strain on my marriage both before and after my diagnosis, between the seemingly endless tests, back-to-back surgeries, and just the sheer amount of what I couldn't do. My husband cared for our daughters when I could not and pretty much took over running the entire house, which caused a lot of resentment. I felt very alone at times. I couldn't always explain how I was feeling, and it was hard for him to truly understand. He felt stuck, watching me be in so much pain and knowing there was nothing he could do about it. Several times he said he would've taken it on for me if he could. By a few months in, the strain really took its toll and there was a point when I thought for sure we would divorce.

The biggest weight on us was the fact that we had hoped to try for a son later down the line, and I had to make the choice to have a partial hysterectomy in January 2016. It was nearly impossible for the both of us to deal with the emotions and hurt, and that my body just couldn't handle another pregnancy. Even though it was hellish at times, Eric stood by me through it all. He tried his best to help out on the days when I just couldn't move. He picked up our daughters from school when the fatigue was too much and I needed to rest, and held my hand through both surgeries as if he was okay, even though it was terribly hard on him too.

It took a lot of mistakes, communication, and an infinite amount of love to get through everything. Now I try to be as honest as I can with Eric about how I'm managing, and when I need help instead of trying to hide my bad days, and he does his best to be understanding even when he feels overwhelmed. We make it a point to spend one night a week with each other no matter what, whether it's watching TV or flowing together. I'm very grateful that he's willing to stick by me, knowing how difficult the road ahead will be, and that another surgery is so close. We truly had to put each other first, even amidst the chaos, and it made a world of difference.

*

SHAUNA COX
Shauna was diagnosed with
endometriosis in 2012 at age 29
My relationships have definitely improved over time, both as a result of my own ability to be more open and honest with what I'm

going through with this disease and as a result of increasing awareness in general concerning endometriosis. When I was younger, for example, I don't think my parents truly understood what I was going through. It probably didn't help that I didn't yet have an official diagnosis. There were many times when they probably thought I was faking it to get out of going to school. Obviously when I was vomiting from the pain, they knew I was telling the truth but there were a lot of times when I was in pain and not throwing up that they would make me go to school. I remember one instance when I was in so much pain and bleeding so heavily that I didn't want to go too far from the toilet. I had already missed school the day before. It was very important to my dad that I do well in school, and he didn't want me to miss a second day. I literally locked myself in the bathroom and stayed there most of the day so I wouldn't have to merge from the relative safety of those four walls surrounding me. Looking back on that scenario, I know that he didn't know how bad it actually was. If he had known what it was like back then, he and my mom would have helped me fight to get the treatment (excision surgery) I so desperately needed.

Today, my relationship with my parents is one of incredible support. Now that I have the diagnosis of endometriosis confirmed, thanks to a laparoscopy, they have done their own research into the disease. They have learned about the pain I can experience at all times of the month, not just on my period. They've discovered that there's a reason why I'm always tired, and they've seen how hard it is for me both physically and emotionally to not be able to get pregnant because of endometriosis.

Once I found out about the Center for Endometriosis Care, my parents generously offered money to help pay if I chose to go ahead with the surgery, as well as stepped up to be mine and my husband's backup if we got stuck financially. They are both retired now, so that's a huge offer to make. Above the financial help though, I know I can always count on them to listen to me vent with anything I am going through, and it helps to know that they truly get it now.

Growing up it was also hard for me to make friends, both because of my shyness and because of the pain and embarrassing situations I'd find myself in due to the endometriosis. What girl wants to go to a sleepover when she could potentially bleed right through her pajamas? There was also the risk that I'd make plans to hang out with someone and have to cancel, yet again, due to the pain I was in. That can only happen so many times before people start thinking you're faking it and just don't want to try to hang out with you anymore.

Now that I'm more comfortable with who I am as a person, I have become a much more open and honest woman. My friends know that I have endometriosis. They know the pain that I go through, and they understand if I have to cancel on them. I find, though, that I can follow through on more plans now that my friends actually know what I'm experiencing. I don't have to be one hundred percent to hang out with them. I can be in pain and feeling sick, and we can just sit on the couch and watch TV, and that's okay. It's relieving to know that, and if anything it helps the pain I go through, to be able to relax in at least that part of my life.

Most importantly the relationship with my husband, Roger, has always been one of support. I am reminded constantly by how lucky I am to have found him to spend my life with. I told him early on in our relationship about my suspected endometriosis diagnosis. He knew that there was a possibility having children might be hard (although I don't think either of us ever really truly believed it would be this hard). He also understood that there would be times where I would be feeling sick, tired or in pain. I've lost count of the number of times he has drawn a hot bath for me when I'm squirming and moaning in pain in bed, trying to get into a comfortable position where I don't hurt so much. There are times where I haven't even had to ask, and he'll offer to go and get the water running for me.

I don't think I even realized how bad I was feeling until Roger pointed it out to me. He told me one day, after I complained yet again about being in pain or not feeling good or being tired, "Tell me when you're feeling good." I told him okay and kept it in the back of my mind, ready to tell him on the first day that I felt great. I went months before I was able to tell him, "Hey, I feel good today!" That helped me to see how badly I need to deal with this.

It's scary to undergo another surgery, but I might need to in order to improve the quality of my life and to give us a shot at our dream of having children. If I didn't have Roger, I don't know that I would have the courage to go ahead with another surgery. He's my rock. While I'm sure he doesn't enjoy hearing me complain about how I'm feeling all the time (hence, why he brought up the idea of me telling him when

I'm feeling good), he hasn't hesitated to accompany me to various endometriosis events two hours away in the city. He came with me to an endometriosis awareness comedy night in the city when he had schoolwork to do, and squeezed my hand during the opening presentation when he saw I was tearing up at the perfect description of what I and every woman in the room dealt with on a sometimes daily basis. He recently drove two hours to the city with me for an endometriosis march, and even wore an endometriosis T-shirt!

Every relationship has ups and downs. But because Roger has seen me through my worst and has stayed with me, I know that together we can get through anything.

*

JORDANNE GOLD
Jordanne was diagnosed with
endometriosis in 2014 at age 22

The relationship that has been affected the most by my struggles with endometriosis has been my relationship with my boyfriend. My symptoms started to affect my life at the beginning of our relationship. Through multiple doctor appointments, mental breakdowns, and hopeless nights of pain, my boyfriend was there every step of the way. Although most of my relationships had been under stress because of my health, my boyfriend and I became closer. This journey has pushed us in ways we could never have imagined. At the same time it showed me how much we truly love each other. My boyfriend walked this terrible journey with me, and I wouldn't want anyone else by my side.

Being with someone on the good days is easy, but being with someone through the bad days shows an honest love. Although the relationship with my boyfriend grew, relationships with a handful of friends disappeared. As sickness changed who I was and who I could be, friends took that as a sign of me turning away from them. In turn, they turned away from me.

*

CHRISTA HALL
Christa was diagnosed with
endometriosis in 2015 at age 24

Having endometriosis has been a challenge in life. I've lost a lot of important people throughout times when I needed them the most. Over the past eleven years, I have lost countless friends because I have been "flaky" or ignoring them. Having a chronic pain disease at such a young age is so isolating. Most teenagers and young adults have no clue what chronic pain is, so when you cannot be present at all times, it makes you incompatible with many people your age, who believe that you can't really be as sick as you say you are all the time. My mom has been with me since the beginning of my journey. She was there with the doctors, angry that they could not understand why I was in so much pain, and comforting when I was lying in a hospital bed. It has definitely given us a closer mother daughter relationship.

My marriage has also been affected. God has blessed me with the most patient and loving man who has taken care of me no matter what. Living with a wife who has a chronic pain disease is not easy. It's hard for me to work full time, as I don't have the energy or capacity to be able to work forty hours a week. Even working part time, I have a hard time coming home from work and being able to take care of the house, cook dinner, and clean up.

Our sex life as well has been affected. Because of the areas that my endometriosis grows, sex is extremely painful and usually causes me to bleed during and after intercourse. But the biggest relationship that this disease has affected is with God. For the longest time, I couldn't understand how a loving God could hurt a person the way that he has. To make any person with chronic pain suffer for days or months on end with no end in sight was so confusing to me, that he would let this happen to any God loving person. Through the years, I've forgiven God for the life that was given to me, and I use my experience to help others who suffer with chronic pain.

*

BETH JENSEN
Beth was diagnosed with
endometriosis in 2009 at age 20

Over the years this has changed, as most relationships grow, although I have lost friendships and employment due to my endometriosis. As a teenager, it was hard to maintain friendships because no one could see what was wrong with me, and I didn't have the answers then. Most of the time I figured I was blowing everything out of proportion and I was overreacting. It was always hard for me to maintain a job as I was always taking sick days, sometimes I would fake having a cold because I was in too much pain curled up in the bathroom from endometriosis, and I knew that my employers wouldn't accept another "female day." This same thing got me into trouble while I was in school as well, I just didn't know how bad it would affect me in my working life.

The biggest relationship strain was with my mother. She never seemed to be able to understand what I was going through. All the doctors she took me to couldn't find anything wrong. The tests they ran all came back negative, and she didn't suffer from this kind of pain. We fought a lot while I was growing up, and it didn't help that she was a single mother and I was quite a secretive teenager. It unfortunately took a pathological report for it to really click with my mother, this was when I was twenty. At that time, I didn't know if our relationship would ever get better, but it did as she read up on endometriosis and did her own research. I'm happy that we are finally closer than we were when I was younger, but I'm also sad that it took so long for us to build a bond we should have had years ago.

*

CARMELA POLLOCK
Carmela was diagnosed with
endometriosis in 1995 at age 25

After the birth of our son, it was my husband who was impacted the most. The monthly pain and discomfort worsened and caused my behavior to change, leaving me feeling terribly sensitive and reactive. Most months I had limited energy reserves, with the majority of what I had given to being a mum, managing a home and working. The endometriosis would take the little I had left, leaving my husband by the wayside.

He mentioned several times that he felt unloved and forgotten. However, at the time, I didn't know how to change my circumstances. Gifted with the opportunity to reflect on the past, I can see how precious and forgiving my husband was. His compassion and empathy for my suffering was deep and meaningful. He held me when my defenses were down, even when I pushed him away. Endometriosis plummeted me down an emotional mountain and stripped me of the ability to feel love. It was my husband who stood at the base of that mountain, embraced my broken body, and refused to give up.

Deepak Chopra wrote, "Hidden in every event of your life is a possible epiphany about love." My epiphany was realizing the depth of my husband's love during the challenging periods of our marriage. My life has been truly blessed with a husband who has an amazing and generous heart. Thank you to my beloved husband for loving and supporting me simply because he believed things would get better.

*

ASHLEY ROMANKO
Ashley was diagnosed with
endometriosis in 2005 at age 21

Every single relationship and friendship has been impacted. My husband and children are most impacted because they live with me and see me at my worst. They see me having to stop doing something because of the pain. They see me in tears because of the pain. They see my depressing moods. They see me when I can't go out with the family because of how bad the pain is. They see me when I can't get the housework done. They see me when I can't do simple everyday things. My husband has to work more because I'm in too much pain to work. My husband has to help more with our kids because of how bad the pain is. He has to help more with our kids when I'm unable to.

*

JACQUIE YOUNG
Jacquelyn was diagnosed with
endometriosis in 2012 at age 22

My relationships have been impacted in many ways. Certain friends I thought I had, disappeared. My family has been incredible with their support. My husband probably understands my illness more than anyone. He's so caring and he helps me when I'm not well. I have also made new friends from having endometriosis. The online support community has introduced me to some incredible women who I can call some of my closest friends. I coped with the loss of my old friends by accepting that real friends are there when you need them most. I surrounded myself with family and that really helped me deal.

*

JENNIFER YOUNG
Jennifer was diagnosed with
endometriosis in 2009 at age 21

I would have to say the most impacted relationship has been with the females on my mom's side of the family. Every female on that side has had trouble with endometriosis and female cancers. They have all been able to relate to what my life has been like, and have been there to give me advice.

CHAPTER NINE

Mental Aspect of Pain

It's not just pain. It's a complete physical, mental, and emotional assault on your body.-JAMIE WINGO

The pain-brain connection is a widely accepted theory that receiving nonstop pain signals results in the brain rewiring in areas associated with attention and mood, making those with chronic pain prone to mood disorders. Further, the brain may not be able to attend to other tasks efficiently because it's preoccupied with pain signals. Did the chronic physical pain from endometriosis affect your mental health?

*

ADRIEANNE BEASLEY
Adrieanne was diagnosed with
endometriosis in 2014 at age 31

The physical pain of endometriosis has affected my mental health more than I ever thought it would. The chronic pain wears on me and it has caused me to develop depression. Several months ago I actually contemplated suicide because I felt hopeless that the pain would ever get better. I never thought I would get to that point, but it's very difficult to live with endometrial pain on a regular basis. I started seeing a therapist to help me to cope with the depression that I have developed. My mental health is a lot better than it has been in the past, but it is definitely something that will be a lifelong journey.

*

SHILOH BRITT
Shiloh was diagnosed with
endometriosis in 2011 at age 22

One of the most important things I've learned is that when the body is ill, it affects everything. Your body will do everything it can to show that something is not right. I believe one of the first signs that there was something big going on became relevant in mental illness.

Around the same time when I took notice of my cycle not quite being what it should be, my mental health began to decline. At the time, I was in my first years of college out of state. I ended up medically withdrawing from school and moving home where I finally got the help I needed. My little anxiety problem that I had dealt with since childhood boomed into panic attacks, severe depression, and even suicidal thoughts and actions. Once these issues were identified and I was on a healthy track, I began to have more of the severe pain that would eventually lead to the diagnosis of endometriosis.

I've never given much thought to the interconnectivity of my body. There gets to be a point when you question your own pain. Is it just all in my head? You have so many symptoms that don't seem to have any relation to one another, so we question everything, especially our mental cognition. We all know pain affects us mentally, so it becomes difficult to ascertain what is real during a flare, and what our mind is having us believe to be real.

Having nearly everyone on the outside question the legitimacy of the pain is no help, either. I found that the most reassuring thing to happen to me was to obtain that endometrial diagnosis, because then I had something concrete to fall back on. I finally knew what was wrong. It had a name, and in that name legitimacy was given to everything I had been going through.

*

SHANDI CLOUSE
Shandi was diagnosed with
endometriosis in 2015 at age 27

It didn't take long for the endometrial pain to severely affect my mental health. I felt like I had been robbed of not just my ability to have children, but of the life I knew and loved. My anxiety and depression worsened, and left me endlessly wondering when another flare would hit. And the constant pain made it impossible to hang out with friends or do things I enjoyed.

Most importantly, it drastically changed what I could do with my family; it broke my heart to tell my daughters that I couldn't do things when they wanted to, or explain that "Mommy was just really sick" when they were late to school for the third time in the same week. The guilt just got worse when it got to a point when all I could do with my husband was sit and watch television, praying I wouldn't fall asleep again halfway through the show.

After my partial hysterectomy, my already severe PTSD got even worse, despite seeing my long-term therapist. I had nightmares nearly every night, was suffering from flashbacks of the miscarriage I had six years prior, and ultimately felt like I was less of a woman. There were many times I had thoughts of self harm; that was a demon that I had conquered eight years ago after a ten year battle, and I'm still proud of myself for not giving in to the urge. Through the support of my husband, a close friend, and my therapist, I was able to find other ways of coping like hula hooping, meditation, and writing about my illness that were more positive outlets for when it all just got to be too much for me to handle.

*

SHAUNA COX
Shauna was diagnosed with
endometriosis in 2012 at age 29

From 2012 to 2013, the pain I experienced due to endometriosis was so bad and so constant that I started feeling hopeless. I felt as if the pain was just going to go on and on forever and that there was no one out there that could help me. It was at this point that I was waking up anywhere from 1 a.m. to 3 a.m., and I would be up for hours, in pain, before managing to fall back to sleep. I would then get up at 7 a.m. to get ready for work, where I would get through the day by gritting my teeth and trying to focus through the haze of Tylenol #3.

I was exhausted from the pain and the lack of sleep. I went into work one morning and started to bawl. I cried and cried. I couldn't stop crying! My boss at the vet clinic called me into his office.

"What's going on?" he asked as I sat across from his desk. I explained what I had been going through, and that I felt like the pain was going to go on forever. I told him I felt hopeless. He encouraged me to take the rest of the morning off to do some research. He told me there had to be somebody out there who could help me.

I did what he suggested. I went home, brushed the tears away, and researched. I was online for two or three hours and then discovered the Facebook group Nancy's Nook. This group changed my life! It's all about evidence-based education surrounding endometriosis. It fights to give women the knowledge that is lacking in the medical community. That is where I learned about excision surgery, and found doctors who do the surgery both in my own country in Canada, and in the United States. I found the Center for Endometriosis Care in Atlanta that will (hopefully soon!) do one more surgery to (best case!) cure me of my troubles. Thanks to the encouragement of a thoughtful boss, I found some hope in a couple of specialists and in a community of people who had the research and knowledge I had been missing.

Since then, I have joined several other support groups including one for Alberta, the province in which I live, and for Edmonton which is the closest city to my home (although still a two hour drive away). I have met other women going through what I go through, and others who are worse off than I am. I have also helped others new to the diagnosis find help at a much earlier stage than I managed to find help. It helps to know that there are others like me out there that truly understand what it's like to have this disease, and to know that I am not alone in this fight.

While I say I felt hopeless, I never got down enough to consider suicide. I know there are women out there that have, and there are women who have gone through with it. I don't know if I would have gotten to that point if I didn't find help. I'd like to think that I wouldn't have simply because of the support I have from my family, friends, boss, coworkers, and especially my husband. I know there are women out there that don't have that support and that haven't found a doctor who can help them. I hope that those women find the help they need before it's too late, and I hope that the medical community gains the knowledge they are lacking to truly help women with endometriosis.

*

JORDANNE GOLD
Jordanne was diagnosed with
endometriosis in 2014 at age 22

The physical pain I experienced because of endometriosis disrupted my mental health in ways I could never have imagined. Once I started experiencing chronic pain, I also started experiencing mental health problems, the first being depression. The pain pushed me into a depression I thought I would never escape, feeling as though the world became fuzzy. I started to feel a constant weight on my chest and shoulders which furthered the constant feeling of drowning. While trying to live through the depression, I started experiencing social anxiety—the thought of being around people made me feel as though I couldn't breathe. I was no longer an extrovert; I was no longer myself. On the rare occasion when I found myself in a crowded room, I would feel myself sink away with irrational thoughts of how everyone would judge me because they could feel how unhappy and depressed I was. I was terrified of being around people and seeing how happy everyone else was, and realizing how unhappy I had been for so long. When my physical health was at its worst, so was my mental health. Thoughts of suicide plagued me from the moment I woke until I fell asleep. I wanted the pain to stop, and for years it felt as though this was the only way to bring it to an end. I relied heavily on my boyfriend during this time. Mentally, he was the only thing that kept me going.

My mental health is now something I must manage along with my endometriosis. Now that my endometriosis is better controlled, my mental health has improved drastically. Just as with endometriosis, my depression and anxiety will be a lifelong journey in which I will move forward one day at a time.

*

CHRISTA HALL
Christa was diagnosed with
endometriosis in 2015 at age 24

When I first started suffering from the pain, it was only during my period. I couldn't understand why my cramps literally brought me to my knees, yet with other girls my age, you never even knew they were on their period! As time went on and the pain became worse, I started getting depressed. By the time I was in high school, my stomach would bloat up to what we call an "endometriosis belly," to where I looked five months pregnant. I was being mocked for looking fat, and between the bullying and the loss of my brother that had happened earlier that year, I tried self harming for the first time. With help from my two best friends, Richard and Kimberlee, I got the support that I needed from them as confidants.

A few years later when I was on Lupron, I had a hard time coming to terms with my disease. My hormones were on extreme ends of the spectrum, and I became severely depressed again. We found that I couldn't work full-time, and I had to go on a medical leave of absence, which made my depression worse because it was a job I dearly loved. Shortly after this realization, I began to cut again, especially after the Lupron injections and when my pain became worse than it ever had.

I didn't want to live a life where I was in so much pain that I could barely function. I was a depressed newlywed wife, and it was affecting my new husband. I felt I was making his life, and the lives of everyone I loved, harder than needed. With the help of my husband and my doctor, we stopped the injections and just monitored me. I never went to a therapist. After a traumatizing therapist I had earlier in life, I've always relied on friends. I knew that SSRIs make my depression worse than it already is, so we decided that would not be a good route to take. I still have times where anxiety and depression rear up, especially if I am having a hard time with constant flares or chronic fatigue, but always get the help I need through my support system.

*

BETH JENSEN
Beth was diagnosed with
endometriosis in 2009 at age 20

It absolutely has affected my mental health. I've looked at the life I have in compared to most people around me, and wished I could be like them. I've wished that I could get up in the morning, have a shower, make myself breakfast, get dressed and go to work all day, make it home and make myself dinner and then relax for an evening, but it's simply not my life.

I still go to bed wishing I just wouldn't wake up in the morning. Getting up in the morning is hard. Not only am I mentally preparing myself for movement, but I am also fighting through the pain that I've woken up to. When I do make it out of bed, I rarely eat breakfast. If I can manage to get dressed and I have employment, I have to force myself out of the house. I have to then struggle through an entire day of the unknown, and when I make it home, I'm so tired that I need to decide between eating or showering because both make me need to sleep, and that's if I even have an appetite for food. This is NOT living, this is surviving with little to no hope of ever getting to live.

My husband keeps me grounded and my son reminds me as to why it's worth it. This is why I wake up to a picture of them every morning, it's my reminder. I've tried counseling but never really found it helpful. I have my close friends who let me talk to them, they are my best mental therapy.

*

CARMELA POLLOCK
Carmela was diagnosed with
endometriosis in 1995 at age 25

Before the diagnosis in 1995, my mental health was affected even though it was never diagnosed as depression. I felt the hopelessness, despair and numbness that is depression. With this, I questioned my logic and the strong intuitive feelings that pushed me toward seeking alternative opinions and tests. The many misdiagnoses and monthly pain sent my head spinning until the day I was informed by a doctor that the pain could be "all in your head." I knew it wasn't, but I questioned my emotional state and thought perhaps he was right. Consequently, I refused to see a doctor in fear of yet another diagnosis meandering toward a hypochondriac conclusion.

In the years following, in my muddled way, I was just hanging on through the hostile territory of monthly pain and discomfort. Many times, I had resigned myself to the fact that this was normal and no more could be done.

*

ASHLEY ROMANKO
Ashley was diagnosed with
endometriosis in 2005 at age 21

The physical pain does affect my mental health. It's extremely hard to live in pain every day without a break. Certain parts of the month are worse than others but most of the time the pain is unbearable. It's exhausting. It's depressing. I'm constantly thinking, what's the point? Should I just end my life to break away from the pain? I always end up getting through it and continue living but there are many who haven't been able to. Many who have lost their battle. Sometimes it feels like I'm falling into a deep hole and I can't get out of it. I have to take one day at a time, sometimes one hour at a time. It's a daily struggle to be in pain.

*

JACQUIE YOUNG
Jacquelyn was diagnosed with
endometriosis in 2012 at age 22

The physical pain of endometriosis affected my mental health completely. I became depressed from feeling sick and not being able to feel like my old healthy self. I was told by many doctors that it was all in my head so that messed with my emotions. I also developed social anxiety. I feared that people would ask if I was working or wonder why I was still sick despite multiple surgeries. Luckily I didn't have feelings of self harm. I talked with a counselor and it really helped me identify why I was feeling that way.

*

JENNIFER YOUNG
Jennifer was diagnosed with
endometriosis in 2009 at age 21

It hasn't been so much that the pain itself has made me want to commit suicide, but more along the lines that it messed with my mental stability. There have been times when I could not keep myself mentally level, and I did have to go on antidepressants to be able to function correctly.

When all you know is pain you don't know that that is not normal. It is not a woman's lot to suffer, even if we've been raised that way.

SUSAN SARANDON

*

CHAPTER TEN

Working with Practitioners

But I had to think to myself that this was normal, because that was the attitude. I was 19 when I went to see my doctor and I was told it was all in the mind.
– HILARY MANTEL

Knowledge, attitude, and practice with chronic pain can make or break the relationships with our medical practitioners. Some are understanding and compassionate. Others have preconceived notions or stigmas about chronic pain. What was your best experience with a medical practitioner? What was your worst?

*

ADRIEANNE BEASLEY
Adrieanne was diagnosed with
endometriosis in 2014 at age 31

My worst experience with the medical practitioner would be with my current gynecologist. She claimed that she has special experience in endometriosis and training in excision surgery, so I booked an appointment to have it done over two years ago. Unfortunately, she did not remove all the endometriosis properly and I since developed many adhesions. My endometriosis symptoms are worse than before my surgery. I am hoping to get in soon with an endometriosis specialist in Calgary, Alberta, to see what they can do to rectify the situation and possibly give me a proper excision surgery. My family doctor has been much better than my current gynecologist, as far as prescribing pain medication and referring me for acupuncture and physiotherapy.

It is very discouraging that there is a lack of qualified doctors available to treat endometriosis in Alberta. If there were, more women would be able to have proper treatment.

*

SHILOH BRITT
Shiloh was diagnosed with
endometriosis in 2011 at age 22

I have had a few. Here are the worst:

1. When my longtime family primary care doctor said it was all in my head and I was just seeking attention. He suggested I see a counselor. When I inquired if there were any tests we could try to see if the pain was outside my head, he insisted again that I was looking for attention and was fine.

2. When I went in for a question on pain management to a nurse practitioner I had been seeing for about a year, she accused me of just wanting to get pain meds. When I expressed my disbelief at

the accusation, she told me our session was over and to pay on the way out. I told her I didn't believe I should be charged for the session. She said that I came in and sat down, so I got charged. I never went back.

It seems as though all my best experiences have occurred by happenstance.

1. I surmise that I would have never found that I had endometriosis if I hadn't gone into that walk-in clinic that day. I don't remember the young doctor's name, or what she did. What I do remember is that she was the first medical professional to believe there was something more going on. She sent me to a nurse practitioner in town with more experience, who then sent me to Harborview Medical Center in Seattle, where they made the diagnosis.

2. Julianne Snell, I also happened upon. We had, quite literally, run out of options. The doctors at Harborview said there was nothing they could do for me, and referred me back to my home town. Julianne is a nurse practitioner specializing in women's health. She herself had endometriosis. My mom and I went in for an appointment to just see what my options were—the pain was only getting worse and I was hardly able to work or go to school any more. Julianne sat with us and laid out the facts, and was the first to believe that a hysterectomy would be the answer. Finally, she helped me to get into a local surgeon who would believe me and perform the surgery. After our initial visit she continued to check up on me. She helped me through not only the physical, but also

the emotional aspects of this surgery. I am forever thankful for this visit and look forward to being a patient for years to come.

3. Post hysterectomy, I was all over the place. I had been between primary care doctors for some time and needed to be seen. Lisa Brodski was who I ended up seeing. Never have I been treated with more kindness and sensitivity.

*

SHANDI CLOUSE
Shandi was diagnosed with
endometriosis in 2015 at age 27

My best experience with a medical practitioner so far has been my gynecologist. He was well educated on endometriosis and performed all the necessary tests and exams during my very first appointment. He always gave me the straight truth of what was going on. He was kind when giving me the diagnosis and went through every detail and answered every question.

My worst was my former primary care doctor; she ignored all the signs of what was going on, refused to listen to how much pain I was in, and even walked out on me a few times, because she thought I was faking it. The minute I was able to, I switched my primary care to a doctor who really is amazing and takes me seriously. He sees that I am doing my best to manage my symptoms, is willing to work with me on my options, and truly goes out of his way to help me with all my illnesses.

*

SHAUNA COX
Shauna was diagnosed with
endometriosis in 2012 at age 29

One of my best and worst experiences meeting personally with a medical practitioner involved the same doctor. It was one of the best experiences because she's the best in my province, and arguably the country. She's a gynecologist, but she is known for excision surgery for endometriosis patients in the province of Alberta. She also works with a colorectal surgeon so that they can operate on patients, like myself, who have endometriosis on the bowel. My fertility doctor who operated on me had said that he couldn't proceed any further because he was afraid of putting a hole in my bowel, so at least now there was hope of a doctor who could operate.

Unfortunately, it was also the worst experience because, even though she's one of the best, she still can't or won't help me and I may be forced to leave the country for effective medical care. She told me she wasn't willing to operate on me until my husband and I were done trying to have kids. She stated that she would likely give me a hysterectomy during surgery (even though a hysterectomy is not a cure for endometriosis!), and so she wanted us to do whatever we could to try to get pregnant before we proceeded to surgery. I now know however, that often times if a patient has effective excision surgery, fertility treatments aren't even necessary to get pregnant. If they are necessary, they have a better shot at working because the inflammation present with endometriosis is gone. In hindsight, had I known that, I would have saved the money I spent on two failed IUI cycles and two failed IVF cycles and spent it instead on surgery in the USA, with the best doctor in the world, to get rid of the endometriosis.

With all I've gone through, I'm not ready to give up on the idea of kids and of living a pain-free life. I sent in my files a few months ago to have a free records review done by the doctors at the CEC in Atlanta. As a result, I had what has become my best experience with a medical practitioner. Dr. Sinervo reviewed my records and called me on the phone to do a free consultation. For the first time, I was able to speak to a true expert in the field of endometriosis, and I discovered that there is still hope. Thanks to the advice and knowledge of the amazing doctors at the CEC, I may go for one last surgery in Atlanta. While the government of Canada probably won't pay for me to have surgery there, taking my medical care into my own hands is important enough that I may have to find a way to go on my own. I know that there is still hope for no more pain and for having children, despite what one of the best doctors in my country has to offer.

*

JORDANNE GOLD
Jordanne was diagnosed with
endometriosis in 2014 at age 22

The worst experience I had with a medical practitioner was prior to being diagnosed, when my symptoms were not controlled and were taking my life away from me. The general practitioner I had seen multiple times told me that the pain was normal, and that there was nothing he could do for me. His attitude made me feel as though my

166

pain wasn't real, and as though there was no hope for me to get my life back. This medical practitioner was not up to date on his knowledge of endometriosis, and because of that I suffered.

Still today, this experience has affected me. I now make an effort to reach out to local medical centers to ensure they have up to date information and resources for their patients.

*

CHRISTA HALL
Christa was diagnosed with
endometriosis in 2015 at age 24

The worst experience I ever had was long before I had heard of the term endometriosis. I was fifteen years old and was in the emergency department with what we thought was appendicitis. After a urine test, bloodwork and ultrasound, they found that my appendix was perfectly fine, so my doctor told me I was having complications from a pregnancy. I was then a virgin, and joked that unless I was "the new Virgin Mary," it was impossible. But in his words, "Every fifteen-year-old girl is having sex, you just don't want to admit it to your mother," who was sitting right next to me.

He proceeded to do three more pregnancy tests, and when they were all negative, he decided to do a pap smear. They attempted to give me medication to relax me, but didn't wait for it to take full effect. He did the exam very roughly, and after he was finished, he told us that I had an ovarian cyst that had ruptured. But worst of all, he explained "The hymen was still intact, so she's probably going to experience some bleeding." We were so appalled by the doctor's behavior. I was in more pain, but it was different from the excruciating abdominal pain. I didn't understand the soreness and the bleeding I was having. I'm not sure if my mother followed up with the doctor or his superior after the examination, as the medication they gave me took full effect, and I never really wanted to discuss it with anyone other than my gynecologist.

The best doctor I had was the doctor I found in Connecticut who eventually became my primary OB-GYN. I was at the point when I was in the emergency department literally every month. I was passing out and vomiting from the pain, and became known as a drug addict at this hospital. I had been telling the doctors that the pain was always with my period. On this particular morning, my husband rushed me to the hospital after waking me up because I was screaming in pain in my sleep. They gave me a double dose of morphine, and I was still in pain. They told me they had a gynecological doctor who was about to leave, but saw my case and wanted to see me. He came in, asked me questions not just about that period, but how my cycles had been over the past few months and if they had always been like this. I finally had a doctor listening to me! I explained I couldn't find a regular OB-GYN because no one would listen to me about my symptoms. I found out on this particular morning, on top of the endometriosis pain, I had a very large ovarian cyst that was rupturing. I started seeing him regularly until I moved from Connecticut. To this day, for friends in that area who are looking for a new doctor, I always recommend him.

*

BETH JENSEN
Beth was diagnosed with
endometriosis in 2009 at age 20

My worst experience was with my first gynecologist. I thought he was wonderful at first, as he was highly respected and had plenty of good reviews. He diagnosed me in 2009 with my first surgery. This was supposed to be a diagnostic laparoscopy but turned into removal of a cyst and cauterization of some of the endometriosis. But I didn't find this out until my six-week postop appointment, at which point he told me that I needed to take Trelstar to make my surgery "stick." It would practically guarantee that the endometriosis would be gone. Of course I believed every word that came out of this man—this was one of the worst mistakes I've ever made in my life, and it's left me feeling hurt and betrayed by the medical community.

My best experience is with my current family doctor. He's young and willing to learn. He always takes my references and materials to heart, and will actually read up on things. He got me into a specialist who performed my excision surgery, and he's helped me deal with the aftermath of those surgeries. Best general practitioner to date, by far.

*

CARMELA POLLOCK
Carmela was diagnosed with
endometriosis in 1995 at age 25

I had been visiting the same medical clinic for over twenty years. They knew my history as well as my parent's and sibling's. For a long time, I felt this was important to ensure continuity and appropriate diagnosis based on the written notes recorded and available to them. Somehow this became unimportant, since neither of the resident doctors concerned themselves to look into the reasons for my monthly pain as indicated in my medical file. I was dismissed, then finally informed, "We can refer you to a psychologist." I became despondent, for I knew the pain was real. The screaming voice in my head kept repeating "They were focusing on the wrong part of your body!" Naturally, I went numb to the medical fraternity, forcing myself through the motions of simply coping with over-the-counter medication and being bedridden on the difficult days.

I am a believer that every difficult situation or event in my life is teaching me a valuable life lesson. So when my way went dark and I relied solely on professionals to find answers, I had forgotten that sometimes the answers are inside me. I needed to empower myself to keep pushing and not resting in a place of hopelessness. It is essential I trust the simple everyday wisdom that comes from my body. It is the barometer of my soul and master of my being.

In time, endometriosis was ready to teach me another life lesson—that the lessons learned in the dark can be breathtakingly beautiful.

I was twenty-five years old and woke one night to debilitating pain and struggling to move. I called the ambulance services and was rushed to hospital with acute abdominal pain and uncontrolled bleeding. I underwent a series of scans and blood tests to determine the cause. The Emergency Registrar who treated me immediately recognized the signs and understood the pain I described. She showed compassion and empathy, and shared her own story with endometriosis. In the twenty hours spent in emergency, I could feel the years of isolation fade away. She had brought compassion into a space I always believed no one understood. My suffering had become a shared one—like two comrades exchanging war stories.

Surprisingly, forgiveness found me as well. I replayed past visits to doctors and felt my emotional heart let go of the anger and frustration from the many misdiagnoses. Peace had come into my being. The Emergency Registrar opened the portal of my wounds that I had secretly shielded and unconsciously protected. She projected me on a path of answers and healing. I am forever grateful to her caring heart and reassuring words. She showed me that hope is important to heal a body broken by pain.

*

ASHLEY ROMANKO
Ashley was diagnosed with
endometriosis in 2005 at age 21

I think my worst experience with a gynecologist was when I was told I would be getting excision surgery and afterwards I found out that ablation was done. I was very upset. If I would have known, I would have cancelled the surgery. In my follow-up appointment, I was told that if I didn't take the hormones being offered, to not come back.

My best experience was when I was actually listened to and believed. When told that I may have endometriosis, I felt relieved to finally have a diagnosis. This gynecologist would take the time to see me whenever I had any questions or concerns. My worst experience with a medical practitioner has to be when I was told the doctor was going to give me excision surgery and decided to do ablation surgery instead. So my best experience has been when I went to see the doctor and he believed me. He showed me compassion and understanding. He listened to what I was saying instead of ignoring me because he was the doctor and knew better than the patient.

*

JACQUIE YOUNG
Jacquelyn was diagnosed with
endometriosis in 2012 at age 22

My worst experience was when I was twenty-two years old. The doctor was supposed to be a specialist, but I found out he wasn't. He did one of my surgeries, and a few weeks after surgery I was in more pain than before. I told him how I felt and was belittled and told that I was cured. I asked him if there were any other factors that might cause this pain. He said my only option after having surgery was to go on this drug that caused menopause. I had read horror stories about this drug (Lupron), and I said no because of the side effects that were not limited to bone density loss, hair loss, weight gain, mood swings and depression. When I said no, he yelled at me saying I didn't want to get better and that I was a drug addict. I never even asked him for any medication to relieve my pain, I simply asked why my pain was still persisting. He not only was cocky, but left more than half of the disease in my pelvic area. I didn't trust any doctors after seeing him. I felt like they were all out to get me. Everything changed when I met my new current specialist. I was so afraid to meet him that I didn't show up to my appointment (which is unlike me not to call). Then I get a phone call and it's him! He said "Hey, we missed our date! Do you have a second to talk to me about when all your symptoms first started? Take me back to the beginning." I was blown away with how personable he was. We ended up talking for an hour and he said he got my medical records that I sent and truly believed he could help me. He saw lots of missed disease from my previous surgery photos. I decided to go in for an appointment and actually keep it. It was life changing and amazing. He ended up doing my surgery and helped me so much. He also led me to a wonderful physical therapist. He not only is a great doctor but has the best bedside manner. The two doctors are like night and day. My best advice is, if you don't like your current provider then switch because there are amazing doctors out there, you just have to look.

*

JENNIFER YOUNG
Jennifer was diagnosed with
endometriosis in 2009 at age 21

There have been a couple of doctors who are right up there on being horrible experiences. The ones who were horrible were an emergency room doctor and a general practitioner. Both times were dealing with cysts. When I saw the emergency room doctor, it was right at the beginning of my suspecting endometriosis. I was actually one of the rare girls out there who was still a virgin. When I asked him to please be gentle, he asked me why and I told him. He laughed at me and told me in front of my mom that I was lying and there were no more virgins out there. He then proceeded to jam the speculum up inside as hard as he could and yank it open. I immediately started crying so hard from pain that I could not make a sound. The second doctor who was horrible was the doctor who was doing the Saturday morning clinic at our primary doctor's office. At this point, I had quite a few cysts that had ruptured before that, I knew what was going on and told him that I just needed pain medicines for it. He asked me if I could be pregnant and I told him no, since I was still a virgin at this point as well. He proceeded to tell me that he was going to do a complete CBC blood and urine test for infections. He came back and before he even got to my room, he was yelling in the hallway that my pregnancy test came back negative and that I was right about cysts.

My best experience was with two other doctors, the first being my doctor who did my surgery. He is a gynecologist oncologist. He really listened to what was going on with me and was prepared to do whatever was necessary, in my best interest. My other doctor was the one who did my hysterectomy in April of last year. He listened to me, didn't shut me down, and understood my reason for being done with this disease, and did what it was time to do.

*

CHAPTER ELEVEN

Engaging in Intimacy

Being able to feel good having sex is what makes me feel like a woman. Having that pleasure taken away and replaced with endometriosis pain is a feeling that can't quite be put into words. -CARLY C

For many, endometriosis results in painful sexual intercourse. For some couples it results in rejection and hurt feelings, and becomes the elephant in the room. For others, it's an opportunity to indulge in creative pleasure. What strategies do you use to help your body experience pleasure instead of pain?

*

ADRIEANNE BEASLEY
Adrieanne was diagnosed with
endometriosis in 2014 at age 31

Pain during intercourse has been an issue for years. In the past couple of years the pain has gotten worse. My husband has learned which positions are the best when I feel uncomfortable. It is a difficult subject in our relationship, and it does make me feel very insecure.

*

SHILOH BRITT
Shiloh was diagnosed with
endometriosis in 2011 at age 22

In all honesty, it got to a point where all that existed was pain. We would try, but the pain would become too intense and I would end up doubled over crying begging to be taken to the emergency room or for a Vicodin. After this became commonplace, I put the brakes on—I was too afraid of the pain. This gave rise to a different kind of pain. I felt as though I was a failure as a fiancée, then as a wife. I believe the mental side of this was far worse than the abstinence we endured during this time. My husband felt as though he was unwanted and unattractive, and I felt as though I had failed him. In turn, I began questioning whether we should be married at all.

I thought that after the hysterectomy the intimacy would return. What I was not prepared for was the psychological effects to last long after my uterus was removed. Today, I still have problems getting over this physiological block.

*

SHANDI CLOUSE
Shandi was diagnosed with
endometriosis in 2015 at age 27

Sexual intercourse was, and still is, a tricky situation for us. In the months before my surgery, intercourse became sparse because it was just too painful or would leave me stuck in bed for days afterwards. If it wasn't the pain then it was the extreme fatigue, the constant nausea, or the fact that the endometriosis flares were causing my other illnesses to flare as well, complicating my already severe symptoms. We found that certain positions were okay on some days, while others were completely out of the question as it would be excruciating for me. We also learned not to put pressure on ourselves about how much or how little we were, as that only made things worse.

Lengthy foreplay and just listening to my body went a long way in helping to make intercourse less painful for me, as I would be in a more relaxed state, and made sure I gave myself plenty of time to rest or sleep afterwards. It took a lot of trial and error for us to figure out what helped and what didn't, and to be honest not much else did. After I healed from surgery, it became significantly easier for several months, though there are still times where we have to add in those things or work around it due to the pain returning.

*

SHAUNA COX
Shauna was diagnosed with
endometriosis in 2012 at age 29

There are only a handful of times when I have experienced painful sexual intercourse as a result of having endometriosis, so I guess in that respect I have been lucky. When I have experienced pain, it's been on deep penetration. Now that we know that can be a problem for me, we avoid positions that cause that. I'm lucky that my husband encourages me to be open with him and to tell him if anything hurts so that we can do something different. He hates the idea of causing me pain, and so at the first sign of discomfort, we either change positions, or he helps me to relax. I find relaxing is the best strategy to ease any pain experienced. Sometimes this means I'll have a hot bath before intercourse to relax my muscles and my mind. At other times, my husband might give me a massage to help me loosen up. The most important thing, though, is communication. If anything is uncomfortable or painful, I tell him and we either do something different or stop. It helps to know that he's so easy going and happy no matter what.

*

JORDANNE GOLD
Jordanne was diagnosed with
endometriosis in 2014 at age 22

Pain with intercourse had been a symptom of endometriosis that I struggled with since the beginning of my journey with endometriosis. The pain would feel like a hot knife, it felt as though my insides were being ripped apart. At my worst the pain was so bad it would make it impossible for intercourse to happen, and after a while the pain had been so driven into my mind that the thought of intercourse was horrifying. After having excision surgery with a specialist and going through months of pelvic floor therapy, I was able to ease the pain and feel good again.

*

CHRISTA HALL
Christa was diagnosed with
endometriosis in 2015 at age 24

I've always bled after sex, but it wasn't until I went off my birth control in 2012, and my endometriosis started growing more, that painful sex became an issue. When it first started happening, I became

178

afraid of sex and was terrified to let my husband touch me intimately. Soon, I started feeling insecure about myself and felt like a failure because I was not able to be intimate with my husband. I told him once that the reason why I was hurting so bad was because of sex, and he worried that he was at fault for my pain. I I didn't want him to carry that burden, and for a while I didn't tell him sex was hurting me.

I had managed to keep a stockpile of pain medication in case of emergency, and began using them to be able to have sex. But it didn't help with the days following when I had severe cramps or felt like I was in the middle of a painful pap smear. I finally came to my husband, explained my situation, and we started to think of ways that we could still be intimate with each other in ways that didn't cause pain. It was trial and error for a while, but we got into a rhythm with each other. We found that vaginal sex was an option during ovulation only. For the rest of my cycle, we had only oral sex. After my surgeries, sex became a bit easier. We can have vaginal sex more than before, and I don't bleed as much after. I still cramp afterwards, but not as severely. My husband has been amazing at picking up signs and body language that my body isn't capable of having sex, as I try to push past it to keep that connection with him.

*

BETH JENSEN
Beth was diagnosed with
endometriosis in 2009 at age 20

In the beginning, intercourse was not painful as long as I wasn't ovulating. I enjoyed it and it kept me close to my significant other.

Over the years, this has changed. We are at the point that we can't have intercourse without it hurting me in some way. Most times, I can manage to keep myself in the positions that keep intercourse from being painful, but as soon as I am about to reach orgasm, and during, it feels like I'm being killed. I've tried training my body to feel good without penetration, but even masturbation gives me pain, and I haven't figured out how to overcome this problem. Usually we just abstain from intercourse because my husband is afraid of hurting me, but I have sexual feelings for my husband and sometimes I just can't stop myself, though it usually leaves me feeling crippled the next day, regardless of how slow or careful we were.

Thankfully my husband is an amazing man and has stuck by me all these years, he understands that our sexual life has needed to change because of my disabilities, and most importantly he still loves me through all of it.

*

CARMELA POLLOCK
Carmela was diagnosed with
endometriosis in 1995 at age 25

My need to love and be loved was and is important. However, prior to my hysterectomy, the fear of pain was far more dominant. Fortunately, I am gifted with a very compassionate, understanding and patient husband. He understood my cycles as well as the discomfort of intercourse. We spoke openly and honestly, and he respected my physical boundaries at certain times of the month.

Together with my husband, we used three strategies that helped make intimacy more enjoyable.

1. I take ibuprofen one hour prior to sex to reduce the pain. This seems to take the edge off.

2. Experimenting with different positions helps. We figured out which sexual positions hurt, and ruled them out. This was also dependent upon where I was in my cycle.

3. Intercourse was better at certain times of the month; one week leading up to a period was too uncomfortable.

*

ASHLEY ROMANKO
Ashley was diagnosed with
endometriosis in 2005 at age 21

Intercourse isn't just painful during and after, it's also painful for the next couple of days. It feels like I'm being repeatedly knifed inside. In the last few years, we've found that if I plan when we do it, and do nothing during the day, the pain is a lot less. I also need to take strong pain medication about forty minutes before, which is how long it takes for the medication to work for me. Gentle foreplay is essential, it helps relax your body and I've found I can sometimes enjoy intercourse without excruciating pain. After intercourse, the pain is worse for a couple of days. Many times, I am in too much pain to engage in intercourse. Sometimes I just can't take any more pain and I know the pain gets worse both during and after. I feel less of a woman not to fully enjoy something that is meant to be enjoyed all the time.

*

JACQUIE YOUNG
Jacquelyn was diagnosed with
endometriosis in 2012 at age 22

Endometriosis has made intercourse extremely painful for me at times. The most helpful thing is to take an anti-inflammatory an hour before. I know sometimes the moment just happens, but my husband and I are very open about my pain. I have sometimes used lidocaine gel and it works. Other times we just try and if it hurts, we try other positions. Physical therapy has been so helpful with the pain. I have felt like a failure at times, because it has gotten so painful that I have to stop. But I am much more in tune with what works for my husband and I. Knowing your limits and being gentle with yourself are key to making it work.

*

JENNIFER YOUNG
Jennifer was diagnosed with
endometriosis in 2009 at age 21

I had to do a lot of foreplay with my husband and use quite a bit of lubricants. We also had to try several different positions. It wasn't very helpful to me when he would push and I just could not do it.

*

CHAPTER TWELVE

Impact on Sexual Identity

No one likes to get her period, but when your femininity carries with it such pain and consistent physical and emotional strife, it's hard not to feel that your body is betraying you. -PADMA LAKSHMI

Sexual identity is how we fulfill the vital need for human connection. But when chronic pain interferes, sexual pleasures easily take a back seat or disappear altogether. When intercourse is out of the question, how does it affect your sexual identity?

*

ADRIEANNE BEASLEY
Adrieanne was diagnosed with
endometriosis in 2014 at age 31

When we cannot have sex, whether it be because of pain or bleeding, it affects me deeply. This is one of the hardest things we have had to deal with in our relationship. My husband sometimes feels like I am rejecting him, but that couldn't be further from the truth. Not being able to have sex honestly makes me feel like less of a woman and wife. It is still an issue that I have a difficult time handling. In the beginning of our relationship, I was worried he would leave me or cheat on me and that terrified me. When we cannot have sex, we have learned to connect in other ways.

*

SHILOH BRITT
Shiloh was diagnosed with
endometriosis in 2011 at age 22

I was a mess. I felt inadequate. I often told my husband that since I couldn't satisfy him, then he should find satisfaction elsewhere, all the while silently begging that he would not. My husband, being the wonderful man that he is, never wavered. He always said that I was not alone in my battle with endometriosis. Though he did not feel the physical pain that I did, he was every bit as dedicated to the cure as I was. Sometimes we forget that we don't have to be strong all the time....there are others to be strong for us.

In a psychology class, I learned that a woman was defined by the ability to bear children. Soon I became consumed by the question of "what am I?" I felt as though I should not be labeled as a woman. I thought of myself more as a non-gendered person, which was difficult, as I had always identified so strongly with being a woman. I had been proud of my features, aside from the typical stomach region.

I felt that my body had turned on me, and this led to a deep depression. What was I? I discovered that so much of my own identity

184

lay with having that stupid uterus. Without it, suddenly I felt gender-neutral, or worse: gender-less. I was an *it*, I told myself...a person of damage...a person at all?

*

SHANDI CLOUSE
Shandi was diagnosed with
endometriosis in 2015 at age 27

It greatly impacted the connection with Eric in the beginning, as we had never had any issues regarding intercourse up until my diagnosis. It was difficult for him not to feel rejected at times, and I felt guilty for not being able to fulfill what I saw as my duty to him as his wife. It was painful to even admit that it was a problem, let alone express it in a way that didn't leave one of us feeling even more jilted.

We learned that frequently checking in with each other to see how we are doing emotionally is a great way to combat that. I consider myself lucky that Eric understands I'm not rejecting him personally, and constantly reminds me that my body is having the issues, not me. We focus on our love for one another instead of our physical needs, which in turn helped our marriage grow stronger. We regularly set aside time for just us through date nights, even if it's just playing video games or watching anime at home. On these occasions, we go all out once the kids are in bed: we pick what we want to do that evening and Eric will make us a late night dinner and bring it into the living room. When I feel up to it, I'll throw something nicer on and do my makeup, but I'm thankful he's perfectly okay with sweatpants and a ponytail.

We are very affectionate with each other and make the most of what we can every day to keep our bond powerful and loving. In retrospect, it was putting the effort into the small moments like this, that really held us together and helped us stay connected through the most difficult parts of this journey.

*

SHAUNA COX
Shauna was diagnosed with
endometriosis in 2012 at age 29

I've been fortunate that intercourse hasn't been a huge problem for me and my husband so it hasn't affected my sexual identity in terms of my connection with my husband. Times when I don't want to have sex because I'm in pain or feeling sick, I'm blessed with an amazingly understanding husband who supports me and understands what I'm going through. He knows I'm not lying if I say I'm not up to having sex, and we'll find other ways to be connected in those times. Often times that means simply cuddling, hugging, kissing, talking, laughing, and enjoying each other as best friends, not just as lovers.

Intercourse has affected my sexual identity, however, in a different way. When I first got my period, my mom told me it made me an "official woman," and my dad told me that now it was especially important that I not have sex because it could lead to having a baby. We are taught that having sex leads to getting pregnant. When you are young and not yet ready for a family, you spend so much effort preventing that from happening. In my case, however, I have been ready now for over six years, and it stings to know that the method in which I was taught should lead to a baby doesn't for me. I can't have the meaningful connection through intercourse with my husband of creating a baby together. Instead, if we do end up getting pregnant, chances are it's going to happen in a lab with other people present in the room while my husband simply holds my hand as our embryo is placed into my womb by a doctor. All of the romance is effectively taken out of the situation.

I have had to learn to let go of the hope that comes with sexual intercourse when all you want is to get pregnant, and instead relax and enjoy my husband in the moment. My future identity as "mother" is thus taken out of the equation, and my identity as "wife" and "lover" needs to be enough.

*

JORDANNE GOLD
Jordanne was diagnosed with
endometriosis in 2014 at age 22

The pain from sex made it impossible for me to have intercourse. The few times I would try to ignore the pain, I would in the end feel like I was worthless. I would be terrified of my boyfriend feeling like I wasn't enough because I felt like I wasn't enough. Although we were not able to be physically close for nearly three years, we made sure to connect through other ways. Mainly we connect through communicating how we feel about each other and through physical touch, such as cuddling.

*

CHRISTA HALL
Christa was diagnosed with
endometriosis in 2015 at age 24

I've always had a hard time with not being able to have sex. For me, sex in a marriage is important, as it's the closest you can be with your spouse, physically and emotionally, and is the deepest and rawest connection you can have with another person. I've always felt as if I am less than a woman when sex is out of the question. It's hard on any couple that can't be sexually active, and especially depressing that I can't have sex due to physical limitations. I feel a lesser woman when I can't have sex. Before I was open about painful sex, my husband felt unwanted and like I was pushing him away, as I was coming up with any excuse to not have sex without hurting his feelings and worrying him. After I opened up communication though, it wasn't a matter of sexual rejection, it was being conscious of what I can and can't handle, and not wanting to push myself past my limits. It's been difficult finding ways to stay connected on such an emotional level, but we found small things like sitting together and holding hands when we're watching television, or cuddling before bed helps keeps us connected.

*

BETH JENSEN
Beth was diagnosed with
endometriosis in 2009 at age 20

This one is confusing for me, as intercourse has been out of the question for a few years now, and even with that being the case I still make love to my husband regardless of how I'm going to feel. I know it hurts him when I lie and tell him everything feels good, even when he's hurting me through loving me. Our love is strong, but I'm not going to lie and say that it's all sunshine and rainbows every day. I'm sure that this has led to plenty of our fights over the years, but we communicate with each other and I don't look down on him for finding ways to please himself.

*

CARMELA POLLOCK
Carmela was diagnosed with
endometriosis in 1995 at age 25

My husband and I are deeply emotional people and experience tremendous joy in the simple things like holding hands or stroking each other tenderly when intercourse is too difficult. We both felt that intercourse is important but not a priority when chronic illness plays a part in our relationship.

The deep emotions we feel go beyond our consciousness. Communication is important in sustaining this connection, as no subject matter or experience is out of bounds. We share our vulnerabilities and experiences, both good and bad, with respect and love. It has taken many years and major life challenges to bring this level of understanding and love to fruition. We have both suffered long-term chronic pain, and so share a compassion which removes the expectation of what should be based on societal standards.

*

JACQUIE YOUNG
Jacquelyn was diagnosed with
endometriosis in 2012 at age 22

When intercourse is out of the question, I'm there for my partner even more. Massage is a great way to connect and sensual touch helps. I don't feel like this has affected my sexual identity. I am very comfortable with my identity, and if anything having to try other methods has strengthened it.

*

JENNIFER YOUNG
Jennifer was diagnosed with
endometriosis in 2009 at age 21

He would get very frustrated with me and we would sometimes wind up in fights over it. I would usually end up in tears and we would go to bed mad at each other over it.

*

CHAPTER THIRTEEN

Sharing Resources

She's standing on a line between giving up and
seeing how much more she can take. -ENDOBODY

Because endometriosis originates in a female's pelvic organs, it can lead to a number of sexual problems including pain, decreased desire and satisfaction, and fewer orgasms. Despite a disorder that clearly takes a toll on our lives, helpful information can be hard to find. What resources did you find for handling intercourse and endometriosis?

*

ADRIEANNE BEASLEY
Adrieanne was diagnosed with
endometriosis in 2014 at age 31

I got no information from my doctor. My current gynecologist hasn't been helpful at all. I've basically had to google information about sex and endometriosis. The Pelvic Expert had a video series that I did watch and one of the videos was about sex, and I did find that helpful.

*

SHILOH BRITT
Shiloh was diagnosed with
endometriosis in 2011 at age 22

When I first met my husband, I was just beginning to realize that there was something wrong with my health. My husband has never known me without this disease. When we became engaged two years later, I had only recently received the diagnosis. Our wedding was put off over a year in the hopes of me finding better health (and to better pay for the expensive treatments). Around the time we were married was when the endometriosis began to be all consuming. We had been married just over a year when I had my hysterectomy.

In all honesty, I did not find any resources. My doctors advised me to abstain if it hurt. I hated to do anything even remotely physical, as I was afraid it would lead to intercourse and I hated to say no and see the hurt in his eyes. He felt rejected and ignored. I felt incompetent and unworthy.

I married my husband on August 16, 2014, during the time of some of my worse endometrial flare ups. In a time of stereotypical regnant lovemaking, there was pain and a general lack of intimacy.

*

SHANDI CLOUSE
Shandi was diagnosed with
endometriosis in 2015 at age 27

I had very little information from my doctor when it came down to resources on intercourse. All I received was a diagnosis for why it was so painful. I searched and searched on both google and support group forums, but there is hardly any advice on the subject.

From my own experiences, my best advice is to just listen to your body and be easy on yourself. If it hurts too badly, then try something else or take a break so you don't push it too hard. On days when it's impossible, spending the evening cuddling in bed with your partner works well in bridging that gap. While intercourse may not always be possible, don't be afraid to explore new ideas and release any guilt you may be carrying.

We found that the most important thing in keeping our sex life alive was to make sure we let each other know how much we loved each other in other ways, even in the littlest expressions, and to be understanding to how the both of us were feeling. I cannot stress how crucial communication is: talk to your partner when a negative emotion arises, and be willing to listen to what they might have to say. When you make it a priority to balance the emotional well-being of your relationship, you open yourself up to receiving and giving a fulfilling love, despite what is physically going on with your body.

*

SHAUNA COX
Shauna was diagnosed with
endometriosis in 2012 at age 29

I haven't sought out any resources for handling intercourse and endometriosis because it hasn't been a huge problem in my life. Unfortunately, I imagine that not much info would come from my doctor, however, in that so many of the doctors I've seen don't know a lot about endometriosis. I'm lucky at least that my family doctor has been willing to learn from me, and asks me questions about what I know, genuinely wanting to learn and accepting that he might not know everything in this particular area. He is in stark contrast to the doctors I've seen that think they know best, and I come to find out later that they're still believing outdated, disproven information.

Based on my experience, however, I think it's important to be open and honest with your partner. Learn with them what's comfortable and what's not, what feels good and what doesn't, what hurts and what's pleasurable. Communication is key! It's also important to think of other things you can do to stay close if intercourse is out of the question, so that you can effortlessly move to those strategies.

*

JORDANNE GOLD
Jordanne was diagnosed with
endometriosis in 2014 at age 22

Unfortunately while dealing with pain during sex, I was unable to find any resources on the topic. My doctor at the time had no knowledge of the topic. It wasn't until I found my local support group that I learned about pelvic floor therapy, which has helped the most. Pelvic floor therapy not only helped with pain during intercourse but also helped my pain overall. Having someone who is trained and knows how to reduce pain during intercourse is extremely important, and for me was life changing.

*

CHRISTA HALL
Christa was diagnosed with
endometriosis in 2015 at age 24

Finding information on sex with endometriosis is not a very easy task. If you google "sex and endometriosis" the only thing they will bring up is why it's painful. When I was younger, I didn't know what to do. I could barely tell my husband what the issue was, who was I supposed to ask? My mom? My doctor? That's one of the problems with this disease though. Because endometriosis involves the uterus and vagina and periods, most people won't talk about it. It was drilled into our heads at a young age that the vagina is our "private area" and we don't talk about it, so most girls and women who are suffering think that it's normal and even talking to your doctor about something as personal as sex is wrong. It wasn't until I found my current fertility specialist that I finally talked openly about painful sex, but I didn't even get much information on how to help. Most of the tips that I have found helpful have come from special endometriosis groups on Facebook, where you can talk about sex. The one thing that I've found is that each couple is different, so there's not going to be the same way to go about having sex from one woman to the next. For me personally, we have found that extra foreplay helps and positions where I can control the level of penetration. If you're having painful sex, I do recommend you still talk to your doctor to see if they have information, but keep an open line of communication between you and your significant other, so you can find what works best for you both and go from there.

*

BETH JENSEN
Beth was diagnosed with
endometriosis in 2009 at age 20

So far I haven't found much, and doctors have been less than helpful with finding solutions. I do have a resource from my support group that I have not tried yet, and I know I need to look into it, but finding other resources are difficult (at least for me). As for advice, all I can say is keep communication open with your significant other. Let them know when you hurt and what hurts you when you're intimate. People can't read minds.

*

CARMELA POLLOCK
Carmela was diagnosed with
endometriosis in 1995 at age 25

The doctors provided little or no advice on the more intimate matters living with endometriosis forces on couples. Literature was scarce, so I just pushed forward, living with hope that each treatment would bring the change needed to live a pain-free life.

Doctors and gynecologists were more concerned with treating the issue of endometriosis rather than discussing auxiliary matters like the impacts on my sex life. I recall raising it on several occasions, only to be politely redirected back to the options of surgery and medication.

From my experiences, I have found that a relationship affected by chronic illness demands conversation and open communication. It may be easier not to talk about it, but rest assured your partner will be concerned for you, and the fight doesn't have to be a solo one. If I was to provide advice to any women struggling with endometriosis and intimacy, my top two tips are:

1. Don't feel guilty for not wanting intercourse. Guilt builds resentment and can erode a relationship. Find ways to fulfill your needs as well as his. Experiment and play—it doesn't have to be about intercourse.

2. I concealed my pain for years which resulted in unconsciously withdrawing from my husband. I recommend sharing your fears and concerns, and being honest and open so you both learn. Tell your partner what you need. Don't expect him to mind read. Sure, he may get upset because he loves you, but the more you share, the better the relationship and understanding about endometriosis and its impacts on your life.

*

ASHLEY ROMANKO
Ashley was diagnosed with
endometriosis in 2005 at age 21

I didn't really search for resources on handling intercourse and endometriosis but I do have some advice. Make sure your partner takes the time to gently stimulate you. You need to be relaxed and also be in the mood. Planning is the key. It helps to do as little as possible during the day of intercourse so you don't experience a pain flare. Personally, I take strong pain medications beforehand. When I felt them kick in, that would be the time for intercourse. If you are tense and concentrate on how bad it is hurting, then the pain will be much worse. If you are relaxed and interested, the pain may stay at bay. Everyone is different and you need to find what works for you.

*

JACQUIE YOUNG
Jacquelyn was diagnosed with
endometriosis in 2012 at age 22

My endometriosis specialist was very helpful with guiding me to a pelvic PT and he was able to give me lidocaine and vaginal valium to calm those painful spasms that happen with sex. My best advice is to talk with your doctor about ways to lessen the pain and make it more comfortable for you. Even cuddling can be sexy, so do things like that and work up to what's most comfortable for you. The right person will understand.

*

JENNIFER YOUNG
Jennifer was diagnosed with
endometriosis in 2009 at age 21

Very little came from the doctor. I had to rely on other ladies who also have endometriosis. The only advice I have is that you just have to find out what works for you.

*

CHAPTER FOURTEEN

Braving Social Advice

I'll do my best to not judge you after the ignorant comment you just made about a health condition you know nothing about. -ENDOBODY

As an invisible and seriously misunderstood disease, a common problem among endometrial sufferers is how to explain to others who don't understand. Some well-meaning people suggest remedies in an effort to help. Others make comments that only inflame the conversation. How do you handle questions and comments from family and friends who don't understand?

*

ADRIEANNE BEASLEY
Adrieanne was diagnosed with
endometriosis in 2014 at age 31

A lot of people think that because I look alright on the outside, I do not have any disease or pain. This couldn't be further from the truth. I've learned to brush those comments off and also try to educate others that even though people such as myself look good, they can still have awful pain, etc. Some of the worst comments are when people don't believe how involved or serious endometriosis actually is, and they just chalk it up to bad period cramps. There is plenty of inaccurate information about what can help endometriosis and I've heard so many people say that getting pregnant can cure endometriosis, or going on birth control can get rid of it. I wish this was true, but it is not. There is no cure!

*

SHILOH BRITT
Shiloh was diagnosed with
endometriosis in 2011 at age 22

This is difficult, as each situation is unique and needs to be addressed in its own way. I found that I would become offensive when I encountered deniers. Many people thought I just wanted attention. My stomach was always bloated to that of a seemingly third trimester mother-to-be. No baby—just endometriosis. Often I would just ignore people's stares and comments. I became thankful to have an apron to cover my stomach while at work. When I was not at work I wore baggy sweatshirts and yoga pants to disguise my figure as much as possible (it's the Pacific Northwest, so socks and Birkenstocks are acceptable year-round).

During this time, I was a university student. I never told my teachers anything until my condition began to affect my coursework. When I did tell my professors, I found that they were understanding and accommodating, and asked what they could do for me.

I found that once the condition *endometriosis* was uttered, it was often met by "Oh… my sister had that," or something of the like. It seemed that everyone knew someone who had been affected by this disease, and because of this, there was sympathy.

There was one instance that I am not particularly proud of when a few girls who had always been snide to me came up and asked when I was going to have that baby. I gave them a sad smile and said, "I'm not pregnant. I'm sick… so sick that I can never have my own children, but thank you for reminding me." They never bugged me again.

*

SHANDI CLOUSE
Shandi was diagnosed with
endometriosis in 2015 at age 27

There have been plenty of times when I've been posed with comments and questions that, although well meaning, were actually really hurtful. It was difficult for a lot of people to understand just how debilitating endometriosis can be at times, and that it's something I'll have to battle the rest of my life. A few I've heard frequently are: "I bet you're fine now that you've had surgery." Or, "I'm just glad it's not cancer." "At least you had your daughters before your hysterectomy." This one is the most painful. Choosing to no longer have children was not a decision I took lightly or wanted to do. It caused a fierce depression, issues in my marriage, and harsh memories of my miscarriage. Every day I have to remind myself that I did the best thing I could have done for myself, and it was the right choice for my family.

The others are just as hard to hear. While I am grateful it's not cancer, it makes me feel like the severe illness that has taken so much from me has been downplayed and stuck in the comparison trap of which is worse. The comment about surgery is equally hard to swallow because when it comes down to it, surgery is no cure. In fact, in some situations it makes endometriosis worse, not better. It's infuriating to know that society still teaches people that it's a fix-all to our problems. If the person is willing to listen, I try to use these situations as a way to educate them about the facts of this disease and what we deal with daily. There have been just as many times when I've had to walk away and distance myself. Since my diagnosis, I've become very vocal in raising awareness about endometriosis in hopes of breaking the stigmas that surround it, and to deal with the hurtful comments in a positive way.

*

PATRICIA CONNELLY
Patricia was diagnosed with
endometriosis in 2014 at age 33

It irritates me, but I blow it off or ignore what's being said. Out in public, I have to bite my tongue a lot.

*

SHAUNA COX
Shauna was diagnosed with
endometriosis in 2012 at age 29

Endometriosis is a term that people have actually heard now, not only because so many women have it and are more open about their diagnosis, but also thanks to some celebrities who have come forward and admitted they suffer from this disease. Unfortunately, there are still a lot of misconceptions.

I think the biggest misunderstanding I've heard people say when they hear that I have endometriosis is, "That's just bad period cramps, right?" It's a lot more than just bad period cramps. I get frustrated when I hear this comment because I feel as if people think I'm just being a baby for complaining about what I've been through, and what I'm still battling every day. It isn't just a matter of popping an over-the-counter pain pill and getting better.

I think the best course of action when hearing comments is to educate people. I explain what endometriosis is, and what it means for me. It means I am tired every day; no amount of sleep makes me feel rested. It means that when I am on my period, I am often crying in pain and nauseous for the first one to three days. On other days of my cycle, I am also often in excruciating pain. This is either experienced as sharp pains, or a dull constant ache in my pelvis, radiating to my right thigh. It means that my dreams of having children may never come true. Several of my organs are fused together and the surgery that can fix it can only be performed by a small amount of doctors who probably are not even in my own country. I tell people all of this so they can understand endometriosis is not just about period cramps.

The other question I've had from people is, "Why don't you just have a hysterectomy? My aunt had endometriosis, had a hysterectomy and now she's cured." This brings up even stronger emotions in me. It is unacceptable that medical students are still taught that a hysterectomy is a cure for endometriosis. It is maddening that women of childbearing years who want kids are told that the only way to stop the pain is to have their uterus removed. Women have believed well-meaning but misinformed doctors, and gone on to have hysterectomies only to be baffled that they are still in pain afterwards. Using myself as an example, I have endometriosis on my bowel. How would having a hysterectomy get rid of the endometriosis? It wouldn't. Yet women and even doctors are still under the mistaken impression that a hysterectomy will cure their problems.

I have handled every misunderstanding, misconception and myth that I've encountered with the same strategy: education. It is only through educating others that we'll be able to fight this disease. Women suffering from endometriosis need to be their own advocates for the best treatment out there: excision surgery. Doctors need to be better informed, have the ability to recognize their own limitations, and refer women to true endometriosis experts when needed. People don't know what they don't know, and I feel that providing education rather than reacting in anger is the best course to move forward.

*

JORDANNE GOLD
Jordanne was diagnosed with
endometriosis in 2014 at age 22

Having a condition that is generally misunderstood by the public often leads to well-meaning yet ignorant comments and questions. Although most of the time I can look past the ignorance and understand that it comes from a good place, some days it wears me down. It chips away at my self-esteem and, over time, makes me question some of the people I have in my life.

The worst comments are ones that insinuate the condition is less complex than what it really is or when comments are made that say the medical community supports inaccurate information. I'll often hear from people who said their doctor told them birth control is the only way to control endometriosis, or that an ultrasound will show if there is endometriosis present. Those comments are hard to deal with because it shows how deeply rooted the myths and inaccuracies are in our society. On good days when I hear comments from others that are well-meaning yet not accurate, I use it as an opportunity to educate and spread awareness of the condition. On bad days when I hear those comments or questions, I end up staying silent. On these days I don't have the energy to feel like I am fighting a losing battle.

*

CHRISTA HALL
Christa was diagnosed with
endometriosis in 2015 at age 24

When I first started publicly opening up about my chronic pain and probable diagnosis, I immediately began getting messages from many of my friends and extended family.

"You need to try this diet."

"You need to go organic."

"You're too stressed out, you should meditate."

Or my favorite, "My cousin's best friend's sister has that and she was cured by her pregnancy!"

At first, I was angry that everyone was telling me how to control my pain. I had tried literally everything I could find on managing my pain. Explaining that there is no cure for my disease, and that I've tried all of those things they suggested upset a lot of my friends, especially the ones telling me that pregnancy would cure me. My endometriosis is the main reason that I can't get pregnant.

It took me a while to learn how to handle these comments. On one of my endometriosis pages, I said how angry I was getting. A sister on the page told me to teach them, not reprimand them. As common as endometriosis is, most people don't know what you're suffering and just want to help. The next day, I posted a picture of my endometriosis belly and a friend asked me about it. I explained what I have, and how it has affected me. About three months after our chat, she emailed me again to tell me that because of our chat, she talked to her doctor and finally had surgery and found endometriosis and adenomyosis. I felt so empowered that my response not only helped my friend, but also that I helped open her eyes to what she thought was normal.

*

BETH JENSEN
Beth was diagnosed with
endometriosis in 2009 at age 20

The things I hear the most but seem to rub me the wrong way are "Get better," or "Get better soon." Both of them hurt because honestly

I don't know if I'm going to get better, I may not. The other one that has been hurting me lately is, "But I thought the surgery was supposed to fix you." Well, yes, of course that was the ultimate goal. Obviously it hasn't worked out that way, so why would you say that to me? I'm very bad at confrontational subjects, so usually I try to divert the topic to something else or just smile and nod where I can.

*

CARMELA POLLOCK
Carmela was diagnosed with
endometriosis in 1995 at age 25

I had not felt motivated to discuss endometriosis with family or friends before my hysterectomy. On those days, when endometriosis discomfort conflicted with family catch ups, I doused my weary body with ibuprofen or prescribed medication and hoped it would take the edge off. On many occasions, I regrettably turned down offers to meet friends because of endometriosis. Some meaningful friends felt it necessary to share comparable experiences with period pain to show sympathy. Depending on the severity of pain and discomfort, I would consciously retreat for I felt there was no correlation.

Over the years, I have come to understand both endometriosis and period pain. The severity of endometriosis pain and impact on one's life is remarkably different from the monthly period discomfort. One is a chronic illness that is debilitating and life altering, while the other is not. Endometriosis slowly eradicated my quality of life both physically and emotionally. I was hostage to the plight of chronic illness, and I struggled to remember life without pain. Only an endometriosis sufferer would understand this. The misdiagnosis of the past and subsequent lack of understanding from doctors on the severity of my endometriosis symptoms left me feeling isolated and fragmented. Despite endometriosis being documented in literature for many years, I feel the social knowledge surrounding women's reproductive health is still poorly understood.

I task myself now to educate anyone who is willing to listen and understand, to the debilitating effects of endometriosis on sufferers and those who support them. Education will gift understanding and compassion, which is paramount in living with endometriosis.

*

ASHLEY ROMANKO
Ashley was diagnosed with
endometriosis in 2005 at age 21

In the beginning I wouldn't understand such hurtful comments. Why is he/she saying such things? How can they hurt me this way? I realize now that they just don't understand. I don't think I would understand if I weren't going through it myself. It's very hard to go through this and not have support. I have a very supportive husband, he is the most amazing man I know. We have our arguments and we both get frustrated, but we love each other.

Some of the comments and questions I get from family and friends are, "Why don't you have a hysterectomy?"

"You don't look sick, why aren't you working?"

"You would feel better if you lost weight."

"What do you do all day?"

If they only knew that newer research has found endometriosis in babies and that hysterectomy isn't a cure. If you have adenomyosis, then a hysterectomy can help because adenomyosis is uterus related, whereas endometriosis is not. I may not look sick because I apply makeup and have had many years of practice faking being well.

*

JACQUIE YOUNG
Jacquelyn was diagnosed with
endometriosis in 2012 at age 22

I find that the hardest questions to answer are "Are you still not working?" and "Are you still sick even after surgery?" I used to avoid social situations because I'd be so humiliated when family or friends asked these well-meaning questions. I had a really great job, and then had to resign due to being so ill. When asked if I was working, I felt as though they thought I was lazy or not sick enough to warrant not working. When asked why I still wasn't feeling better, I felt like a failure. Most people have surgery, and once they heal they do much better. A lot of my surgeries have helped somewhat, but I still struggle with the endometriosis being chronic. Now instead of avoiding the situation, I explain to others why I cannot get a job at the moment. I tell them it's literally a full-time job going to all of my appointments (specialist follow-ups, physical therapy, chiropractor, etc.).

*

JENNIFER YOUNG
Jennifer was diagnosed with
endometriosis in 2009 at age 21

The comments that I had the hardest time with were when I got accused of just being lazy when I couldn't do something or that I didn't look sick, so how could I have no energy? Another one was their friend's cousin had endometriosis and it went away just by getting pregnant. How about, "Take some Midol.....that will help you with your pain." Sometimes I could calmly explain why those suggestions would not work in my case. Other times, I have just had to walk away and go to where no one could hear me scream out of frustration.

*

CHAPTER FIFTEEN

Finding Support

Surround yourself with people who provide you with support and love and remember to give back as much as you can in return. -KAREN KAIN

When living with chronic pain, support can play a significant role in our ability to manage the challenges. The people and organizations who understand the journey, and offer compassion and care, can become true lifelines. Where do you find the most support for living with endometriosis?

*

ADRIEANNE BEASLEY
Adrieanne was diagnosed with
endometriosis in 2014 at age 31

I find the most support with my husband. He helps me get through the daily emotional struggles and is there to just listen to me. He has been there for me through everything, as things have gotten progressively worse over the years. I love him very much for all that he has done for me during this difficult struggle. I have also joined a couple of Facebook groups, but the one that has offered me the most support is a local group. They offer so much information and support for women living with endometriosis. I am so grateful for all of the resources they provide.

*

SHILOH BRITT
Shiloh was diagnosed with
endometriosis in 2011 at age 22

The most support has always been from those closest to me. After I began opening up about what was going on, my coworkers became supportive even if they didn't understand; sometimes I think their understanding was more pity than anything. My boss was always a great support. Above all else, my mom was there for me. If she hadn't had faith in me, I would likely still be looking for answers. My husband has always been my greatest support, since I first confided in him that something was not right, through the failed treatments and ultimate hysterectomy, onto the present—he has been there for me.

*

SHANDI CLOUSE
Shandi was diagnosed with
endometriosis in 2015 at age 27

My biggest support has always been my husband, Eric. He encouraged me to find a doctor who would listen, took the time to educate himself, and never once let me give up. When the pain took over, he was right there to carry me to bed and get my medications, he made sure I even properly ate when I couldn't, and he stepped up to take care of our girls when I couldn't function. It took waking up from both surgeries to see him by my bed, holding my hand with tears in his eyes, to really understand the level of devotion we have for each other. I have a myriad of health problems and other illnesses, but the diagnosis of endometriosis has been our toughest battle as a couple, and I truly believe that it was his strength that ultimately carried us through the darkest hours.

My younger sister Kayla was also a huge part of my support system. She would drive the thirty minutes to my house a few times a week, and texted me nearly every day to see how I was doing. She would show up with a bag of toys and coloring books for our daughters, and we spent hours together just watching Netflix and talking because she understood that most days I wasn't capable of much else. We were already very close and even though she has her own health issues to deal with, she went out of her way to let me know she was there for me.

They both tried their best to support me, but there was still that gap that they would never be able to fill because they personally didn't have endometriosis. I was lucky enough to be a part of a Facebook group called "Spoonies that Flow," which was a chronic illness group centered around people who engaged in the flow arts, such as hula hooping. It was here that I met the owner of Hoopus: WereWolf HopeCraft, Josie, and her friends Rachel, Sophia, Christina, and Dee.

I later on joined them in helping others to use flow arts as a positive outlet. The group was filled with other women who had similar experiences with endometriosis, and when I received my diagnosis, Rachel and Sophia stepped up to help me through it. We became close, giving advice on what had worked for them and options to try, and even aiding me in some of the toughest decisions on surgery. Overall, I was immensely blessed in the support system I had and I couldn't have done it without them.

*

PATRICIA CONNELLY
Patricia was diagnosed with
endometriosis in 2014 at age 33

I talk a lot to my endometriosis sisters on Facebook. When I'm frustrated or irritated, the sisters help me calm down.

*

SHAUNA COX
Shauna was diagnosed with
endometriosis in 2012 at age 29

I am lucky to have found support for living with endometriosis from a wide variety of people and places. The biggest support has always come from my husband and my parents. While I have also found support from friends and online, nothing beats the love and support of family and from the love of one's life. My parents have been there for me through it all. They have seen me through intense pain episodes where I've been delirious, crying, vomiting and close to passing out. When I lived with my parents, every month my mom would warm up hot water bottles for me. She would help me prop myself up in bed because lying down hurt more than sitting up. She has as weak of a stomach as I do, but she would faithfully empty my puke bucket for me month after month when I was sick from the pain. Today my dad will still send links he found on doctors, treatments, and studies. I know that no matter what, they will be there to help me in whatever way I need. Even if I don't always need them, it helps to know that they're there.

On the first date with my husband we went bowling, watched a movie and talked for hours. I don't think there's a subject that we didn't touch on, including my (at the time suspected) endometriosis. From day one, he has been my rock. I couldn't have asked for a better man to spend the rest of my life with. When I'm in pain, he's there to do whatever I need, whether that means drawing a hot bath, warming up a hot pack, bringing me pain medication, or simply sitting with me and rubbing my back. Now that endometriosis has potentially robbed me of my dreams of motherhood and his dreams of fatherhood, he has been the strength I need even when he is sad about the same loss. He constantly reminds me, "We are in this together," and that I'm not alone. No matter how hard it is living with endometriosis, I can't help but think how lucky I am in life to have found him.

Friends, coworkers and my bosses have been another source of support. My friends and coworkers know about my endometriosis, and it helps when they take the time to ask how I'm doing, and to know that they genuinely care. My bosses have been incredibly supportive as well. They gave me the advice to seek out second and third opinions, and to do whatever it took until I found someone to help me, and they understand if I need to take half a day or even a full day because of pain. I am lucky to have found a place of employment that understands and believes what I experience on a daily basis. I find it easier to go to work every day knowing I have that support.

Finally, online support groups have been a huge help to me in my journey with endometriosis. It helps to know there are so many women out there that truly understand what I am going through because they are going through it too. I have learned so much in these groups, and been given access to evidence-based research that I may not have found otherwise. I live in a small community two hours from a city, so it is hard to go to an in-person support group for this disease. Having online support groups with caring, intelligent women is the next best thing to in-person support, and it is something I encourage every woman with endometriosis to find. In some ways it even beats in-person support. I can't count the number of times I've been up at 3 in the morning in pain with no one to talk to (short of waking my already too understanding husband), only to find someone up at the same time in one of my online groups.

Support is definitely an area I've been fortunate with, and I hope other women with this disease have at least one person or forum in which they can find similar support. It helps to have people to talk to, vent to, and cry to. If you're really lucky, maybe you'll even find at least one person in your life who will be willing to empty your puke bucket!

*

JORDANNE GOLD
Jordanne was diagnosed with
endometriosis in 2014 at age 22

When symptoms first developed, I found support through my boyfriend, as well as my parents. As time went on I found support through research. Being a university student I felt compelled once I was diagnosed to understand the disease inside and out. My research led me to understand every scientific fact about the disease and I realized how much misinformation there was in the world. This gave me the tool to know what was going on inside my body, and what was going to actually help and make a difference. Once I started researching the disease, it led me to online support groups on Facebook. These support groups helped me to connect with others and helped me understand that I was not alone.

*

CHRISTA HALL
Christa was diagnosed with
endometriosis in 2015 at age 24

As soon as my doctor talked to me about endometriosis, I searched for Facebook support groups. He explained to me that not many people have this, so I was surprised by the amount of groups I found just by typing "endo," and was even more surprised by the thousands of members in each group!! There were groups for different reasons: trying to conceive, lesbians, by state, by region of the country and the world! I learned so much more information by talking with these women, more symptoms that were blown off, or women that were told that it was from another disease was actually symptoms of endometriosis.

In addition to the outpouring of support from my Facebook groups, my family and close friends have been amazing, my husband and mother especially. On top of needing support from other sufferers of endometriosis, a physical support system is important as well. Both of them have sat with me at countless emergency room and doctor visits. Even being there when I'm flaring and need someone to help me with daily tasks. My best friends Richard and Kimberlee have also been the best when it comes to my support. They've not only given me trusted confidants, but have sat with me after surgeries, comforted me during my darkest times and have given me an unfaltering friendship throughout the past ten years.

*

BETH JENSEN
Beth was diagnosed with
endometriosis in 2009 at age 20

The most support I have found has been with my friends, depending on who I am talking to the most at that time. As I have aged, my friends have changed and I can honestly say that now that I'm older I know which friends I can safely confide in without feeling like our relationship has changed because of it.

I also have my wonderful support group, which I found through social media. Over the past few years they have taught me which doctors I should see, and which ones I should avoid. They have taught me about my disease. Most importantly though, they remind me that I am not alone in this battle, and they keep me wanting to fight to make things better for the next generation.

I have to say, though, that the number one best support I get is from my husband. I have been with this wonderful man for ten years and he has seen me get progressively worse, but has always been there fighting right alongside me, and helping me have a backbone when I needed it but didn't have the strength. I love you Jens Jensen, to the moon and back—all the love in the world.

*

CARMELA POLLOCK
Carmela was diagnosed with
endometriosis in 1995 at age 25

Internet and accessibility to free social media platforms like Facebook did not exist in the early days of my endometriosis journey. With the inception of the world wide web, the world of endometriosis research became available at my fingertips. I began to search for websites on endometriosis and speak to other sufferers through the embryonic forms of social media.

Doctors and specialists provided some useful information, but I always felt real understanding came from people with lived experience. Sharing my story is cathartic, as it takes me out of isolation and confirms that indeed, I am not alone.

My husband was the one person with whom I shared my thoughts and feelings. With the regularity and certainty of pain, he knew what to do. A warm blanket, hot water bottle, and medication were arranged. He gave me time to rest as he took on the housework and entertained our little boy, ensuring I had breathing space to allow the medication to kick in. His laid-back approach to managing the difficult moments in life always gave me comfort. He simply understood and arranged life, so I didn't have to sweat the small stuff. He allowed me to bring my focus to controlling the pain through rest, and through the warmth of his compassion and understanding.

Before my hysterectomy, I would often seek nature's council as a form of comfort. Observing nature, particularly a scene too beautiful to capture in words, would fill the emotional crevices left by endometriosis. Once I made the decision to have a hysterectomy, the feelings of grief and loss became all too consuming despite knowing that life would be physically better. Sitting out in nature gifted me a quiet purpose of calming my mind and heart, allowing the subtle release of emotional pain that had wedged so heavily on my heart.

*

ASHLEY ROMANKO
Ashley was diagnosed with
endometriosis in 2005 at age 21

I find the most support for living with endometriosis from some of my family and friends and Facebook support groups. I started an endometriosis support group on Facebook with Brandi CK La Perle (Alberta Endometriosis Group), and she is one of the most amazing women I know. She's done so much for the endometriosis community.

I've met many amazing women with endometriosis that I probably wouldn't have met if I didn't have the disease. I'm grateful I've had the opportunity to meet them and become friends with them. They are the strongest women I have ever met. I would have never understood the battle we go through without actually going through it myself. I want to help others with endometriosis. I don't want my daughter to have to experience the poor treatment we are given. I don't want her to deal with any of this. I will be there for her if she does, but it would be nice to have better treatment or a cure.

My husband has been supportive from the beginning. He is my rock. He tries to understand what I'm going through, but it's hard to really understand unless you yourself are experiencing it. He sees me at my worst and he sees me at my best. He is the most patient man I know, and I love him so much. He is an amazing father. I understand that it's frustrating for him to have a wife who needs help with everything. I am thankful to have him in my life.

My sister, Kerstin, is very supportive. I can explain to her how bad I'm feeling and how awful the pain is, and she really cares. She asks me how I'm doing. She encourages me, shares her frustrations about her life with me, and shares her happiness with me. She tells me funny stories and just tries to be there for me. Thank you so much!

My mother is the most amazing mother in the universe. She is supportive and tries to understand what I'm going through. Sometimes we are abrupt with each other, but we are trying to enjoy each other more. When I explain to her how the pain feels she will be show me empathy. It feels like she understands. It's hard for her to see me suffer, and she helps me when she can. She has taken me to surgeries or to the hospital, looked after my children any time I need her to. In the last few years she has retired and moved to BC. I'm happy for her, but I miss her and how much she was willing to help me.

*

JACQUIE YOUNG
Jacquelyn was diagnosed with
endometriosis in 2012 at age 22

I find that the most support I get is from my husband, my mom and an online support group on Facebook. The group actually helped me find my amazing endometriosis specialist as well as introducing me to women whom I can call some of my best friends. It's so incredibly comforting to talk to others about something that affects so many aspects of your life. My friends get it. We laugh, we cry and it just makes this journey so much more manageable.

*

JENNIFER YOUNG
Jennifer was diagnosed with
endometriosis in 2009 at age 21

The most support has come from family members and some of the Facebook groups I am in. Those are places that I can vent my frustrations, and they will completely understand and listen without judgment.

*

CHAPTER SIXTEEN

Confessing Our Struggles

Life is made up, not of great sacrifices or duties, but of little things, in which smiles and kindness, and small obligations given habitually, are what preserve the heart and secure comfort.
-HUMPHRY DAVY

Endometriosis has been called a riddle wrapped in a mystery inside an enigma. It is somewhat of an orphan disease that falls across several different medical specialties resulting in confusion, myths, taboos, and sometimes permanent damage. At the root of it all is a woman in pain. What has been the hardest aspect of living with endometriosis?

*

ADRIEANNE BEASLEY
Adrieanne was diagnosed with
endometriosis in 2014 at age 31

The hardest aspect is dealing with the daily pain. I've tried everything to help including Reiki, yoga, acupuncture and massage.

The pain has affected me mentally and can be quite exhausting. Physically, I am not able to do everything that I would like to, as the pain can be quite bad some days. The severity of my pain and the unpredictability of a flare is one of the worst aspects of this disease. Sometimes it can be difficult to plan things, as I do not know how I will be feeling or if the pain that I am in will be bearable enough. One thing that I can recommend to others with endometriosis is to accept the help and support of people around you. Handling this disease cannot be done on your own, that is just too exhausting and overwhelming. Attending support groups and confiding in others certainly helps.

*

SHILOH BRITT
Shiloh was diagnosed with
endometriosis in 2011 at age 22

Today, after having undergone a hysterectomy on February 5, 2016, it's dealing with the fact that I cannot have children. I become emotional when I spend time around pregnant women or newborns. I loathe checking Facebook to see all the beautiful families. I feel broken. Though this has gotten better with each passing month, still the burden remains.

Perhaps the hardest part is knowing that to have a hysterectomy was ultimately of my own choosing. I did this to myself, and I will always have to live with that.

*

SHANDI CLOUSE
Shandi was diagnosed with
endometriosis in 2015 at age 27

When my journey with endometriosis first started the hardest challenge was to be easier on myself. I was horrible about making myself rest when I needed to, even with my other chronic conditions, and I would run myself ragged no matter how badly I was hurting. Ultimately, it came down to guilt. I felt worthless, especially when it was difficult for people to understand what was wrong with me and why I wasn't capable of doing the things I used to. Or, even worse, when they didn't believe how bad it really was. I tortured myself over the memories I was missing out on with my daughters the most. It turned into a gridlocked cycle of constantly pushing past my limits, which just led to being in more pain and becoming even sicker than I was. My body couldn't handle that kind of pressure on top of the pain. I was mentally exhausted, and spiritually I was running on empty.

Finally, my husband sat me down one day and demanded that it stop. I was doing more harm than good. I was essentially losing who I was. I had to relearn to put myself first—that to do the things I want and need to as a wife and mother, I have to listen to my body when it says enough is enough. Just because I can do certain activities one day, doesn't mean that I will be able to do those same ones the next day. I never know from day to day what my body will be like, so self-care is essential. I bring this up because I want others who are struggling with endometriosis to know you don't have to put yourself last due to judgments from friends and family. Learn from my mistake. Surround yourself with loving friends and family who will support you and want what's best for you, even if they don't fully understand what it's like. Don't settle for a doctor you have to justify your pain to. It's worth seeing a thousand doctors just to find one who will listen and work to help you. You are your biggest advocate.

If I could say just one thing to people without endometriosis, it would be to please understand that not all chronic illnesses are visible. If you see me dressed nicely and in makeup at the school PTA meeting, don't assume I'm suddenly cured. Instead of shaking your head in disgust when you see me climb into my car with a handicapped placard, ask me about my diagnosis. Stop and think about what you would want others to do for you if you were in my shoes, before making assumptions. Every day I fight to make the best out of my life despite the pain and challenges I face, just like everyone else does, and I shouldn't have to look sick or disabled for my struggle to be considered real enough.

*

PATRICIA CONNELLY
Patricia was diagnosed with
endometriosis in 2014 at age 33

The pain, dealing with the pain. The stupidity of others who have no clue what I'm going through.

*

SHAUNA COX
Shauna was diagnosed with
endometriosis in 2012 at age 29

It's hard to pick one aspect that is the hardest about living with endometriosis. In the past, the hardest part was definitely the pain that comes with this disease, especially when my pain was severe and relentless, every day and night for almost a year! However, now that my husband and I have been trying to conceive a child for over six years, and my pain has lessened compared to what it once was, I would say that, now, infertility is the hardest part of having endometriosis.

Since I was a little girl, I have dreamed of being a mom and having a big family. I knew from researching this disease that infertility is fairly common among women with endometriosis. While deep down I knew that was a possibility, I never let myself really believe that I would never be a mom. Now that the possibility of being childless is very real, it's sad and scary. I don't know what my future will look like without kids. I've never imagined a life without children. While I know I will find a way to be happy, and that I have so much to be grateful for in my life, it is still hard to bear. It is hard thinking that this disease has taken a big part of what it means to be a woman away from me. It has taken our choice of children, mine and my husband's dreams for our future, and crushed it.

I was diagnosed as having stage four endometriosis and told that my chances of conceiving are low. I have already undergone two intrauterine insemination procedures and two invitro fertilizations that have failed. My last course, which I wish I knew about sooner, is to go for excision surgery in hopes of improving my fertility. It will, hopefully, also have the added benefit of getting rid of my pain and helping me to feel more rested and alive again. I am tired of constantly feeling exhausted, but I would take the tiredness and the pain in a heartbeat if it meant that I could have a baby. At times I feel guilty thinking that because I know there are women suffering every day. I used to be one of them. I know that when the pain was that bad, and when it was seemingly never-ending, in that mindset all I wanted was to be rid of it, even if that meant being childless.

As such, I want people to understand that endometriosis is different for everyone. It is also different for each person at different times in their lives. When the pain is a ten, all you want is for the pain to end. When the pain is that bad, you would give up anything for it to stop. On the flip side, when the pain subsides enough to live a little, if you want kids all you care about is getting pregnant, even if it means giving up the ability to get through the day without popping a pain pill, or grinning and bearing it. Endometriosis is experienced so differently among women, and yet we are all in this battle together. The challenges change from day to day, week to week, month to month, and year to year. But ultimately, whether we are dealing with the pain, the infertility, the tiredness, or any other of a number of symptoms that go along with this disease, it is important to never give up and to know that there will come a day when things will be better.

*

JORDANNE GOLD
Jordanne was diagnosed with
endometriosis in 2014 at age 22

At the start of my journey, I found the hardest aspect was communicating what was going on with my body. I was constantly in pain and had no way of explaining why it happened and why nobody knew about it. It was also very challenging getting past the stigma of endometriosis and talking about periods and menstrual cycles. People didn't want to listen to me talk about my condition because it made them feel uncomfortable.

The hardest aspect of living with endometriosis at this point in my life is having people in my life who don't understand what I have been through, or how it has changed me as a person. The relationships I had prior to going through my journey are still strained. Those friends could not see what I was going through or how I was growing as the pain changed me.

If I could share my experience with others, I would like them to know how hard it is to pretend that your chronic illness isn't there. It is emotionally draining to have people in your life that do not want to recognize the other half of you which is fighting a war. When you are going through chronic pain or a chronic illness, you need everyone in your life to be on your team, which means everyone who is a part of your life needs to recognize and understand the battle we are going through.

*

CHRISTA HALL
Christa was diagnosed with
endometriosis in 2015 at age 24

The hardest aspect of living with endometriosis for me would be the lack of control of my symptoms. My pain and fatigue flares at any given time, which makes me unreliable. I can't always work when I'm needed, I even had to go on a medical leave of absence from a job I loved because of my disease. I've lost friends because I'm not available at all times or because I've missed important dates. It took me years to not hate myself and blame myself for a disease I have no control over. Over time, the feelings of resentment went away, but were replaced with depression. I was learning how to live not like a normal woman in her twenties, but rather a woman who has to constantly monitor my body and how I'm feeling, and judge just how long my energy levels will maintain. After a while, I stopped going to hang out with my friends and chose to text because it took less energy, and after a while that was not enough for some. I've had to learn to put my health first, because I can't help anyone if I'm not at my best.

*

BETH JENSEN
Beth was diagnosed with
endometriosis in 2009 at age 20

The hardest aspect for me is remembering what it was like to wake up with a full day of potential in front of me without a care in the world, when I'm now living in daily pain and fatigue at only twenty-seven years old.

*

CARMELA POLLOCK
Carmela was diagnosed with
endometriosis in 1995 at age 25

The decision to have a hysterectomy, despite the fact that my childbearing years had not clocked off, proved the most difficult and tested my emotional endurance. Leading up to the surgery, I learned courage and the importance of self-love, as the surge of emotional pain and guilt became more agonizing than the physical pain of endometriosis. I felt cheated out of my reproductive investments as well as failing to fulfill my husband's desire to have more children. It was this that hurt the most.

The world needs to understand the expectation that a woman should easily conceive and carry a child to full term is a recipe for resentment and grief. Society and family expectations set up an endometriosis sufferer for thinking she is taking a wrong turn and to feel cheated out of what she deserves. I became exhausted from the expectation that led to grief and resentment of my body.

In my late thirties, I stopped trying to convince people that the pain of endometriosis is, in fact, real. For too long I felt the need to validate my pain with doctors, family and friends. I look back now and shake my head, as the struggle should not have been there. I felt the pain surges and spasms that left me hunched over. They were real, it was real.

With hindsight, and from living the many physical and emotional challenges of endometriosis, I learned the importance of teaching my mind to be kind to my physical and emotional self. Beating myself up because I wanted to free my body from pain is no way to exist. After twenty years with endometriosis, I have come to understand that perhaps the greatest life lesson is learning how to accept the journey fully, to embrace my choices and love myself unconditionally.

I did the inner work to uncover the simplicity of healing by releasing the expectations that had sabotaged my emotions for so many years. I am now not afraid of being human and flawed. Endometriosis challenged my existence but allowed me to see that perfection is indeed messy and unrealistic, and so redirected my journey to self-love and acceptance.

*

ASHLEY ROMANKO
Ashley was diagnosed with
endometriosis in 2005 at age 21

Personally, the hardest aspect of living with endometriosis is the pain and the misunderstanding toward it. It's hard to be battling every day and then have someone not believe how much pain you are in. I'd like others to know that I am in as much pain as I say I am. I want others to know that it's okay to be supportive and understanding even when you don't understand it yourself.

*

JACQUIE YOUNG
Jacquelyn was diagnosed with
endometriosis in 2012 at age 22

The hardest part of living with endometriosis, aside from the physical pain, would be the feeling of being misunderstood. The misunderstanding is very dangerous when it comes to doctors. When doctors don't understand your disease, symptoms, etc., it can delay treatment. They may brush you off and leave you to fend for yourself. It happens to so many women, including myself. The other part of being misunderstood also applies to social situations. It can be very isolating in daily life when others don't understand what's going on with you. Over time the pain was my biggest challenge, but honestly connecting with others who don't have endometriosis has been difficult for me. I want others to know that even though your friend who has endometriosis did things the day before, that doesn't mean she isn't suffering. A chronic illness has many aspects, and how we feel can vary from one minute to the next. Also, I would like others to know that the pain is debilitating. We are very good at looking healthy, so all we want is compassion.

*

JENNIFER YOUNG
Jennifer was diagnosed with
endometriosis in 2009 at age 21

The challenges that I have had to face that have been the hardest for me is that there is no cure for endometriosis and that I will be stuck with this all my life. It was also hard for me to swallow that the two kids I have are all I was physically able to handle, and even that was barely. One other thing that is hard for me emotionally and mentally is knowing that there is a good chance that this endometriosis might get passed along to my daughter. It is very hard for me to swallow the thought of her being in so much pain, and knowing there will be nothing I can do about it when that day does come.

*

CHAPTER SEVENTEEN

Finding the Silver Lining

Even a small star shines in darkness.
-FINNISH PROVERB

On any journey involving chronic pain, the thought that anything good can come from our experience is beyond comprehension. Yet we all carry wounds of some sort which, no matter how large or small, leave us with the instinctive need to find the hopeful side of the hand life dealt us. It's human resiliency at its finest. Have you discovered a silver lining from your journey with endometriosis?

*

ADRIEANNE BEASLEY
Adrieanne was diagnosed with
endometriosis in 2014 at age 31

This journey over the past few years has been extremely difficult. The silver lining that I have discovered is that I am able to help other women who are going through a similar experience. I am very vocal about my endometriosis on social media, and there are many women who have privately messaged me asking for advice or more information about it.

Endometriosis has also made me more aware of my own health, and I now live a much healthier lifestyle than I had prior to my diagnosis. It has changed me as a person, both mentally and physically. I have learned so much more about my body than I could have ever thought possible. I listen to my body so much more now. When I am having a good day, I definitely take advantage of it and do as much as I possibly can because I never know when a really bad day will come and render me incapable of doing anything.

*

SHILOH BRITT
Shiloh was diagnosed with
endometriosis in 2011 at age 22

Living with endometriosis has taught me how strong I am... and how, with the backing of family I am even stronger. Additionally, the experience has proven that my young marriage can get through turbulent times. My husband and I often joke of having gotten through the "worse and sickness" and are on to the "better and health."

*

SHANDI CLOUSE
Shandi was diagnosed with
endometriosis in 2015 at age 27

The silver lining was that being so sick proved just how strong I really was, not just physically, but mentally and spiritually as well. At first, my diagnosis was a heavy weight on my shoulders that would never be lifted, just another cursed chronic illness to add to my already long list. While I've never been the type to give up, I crumbled under the pressure of endometriosis for a while. Along with the pain wearing down my body and mind, my spirit had been broken, and either I could continue to give in or I could stand up swinging. So I stood up and took my life back. It's taken months of soul searching, but in allowing myself to shatter for a period of time, I figured out there was a strength inside that I had no idea I had. Endometriosis may be tough, but I know now that I am tougher.

*

SHAUNA COX
Shauna was diagnosed with
endometriosis in 2012 at age 29

There are a few silver linings that have resulted from my journey. One is that I've discovered how tough I am, both physically and mentally. If someone had told me years ago how much physical pain I could handle, I would never have believed them. I have wanted to get a tattoo for so long, for example, but didn't think I could deal with the pain. After going through endometriosis, I knew that I could do it, and have since gone for a couple tattoos, and hope to go for another one to symbolize my journey with endometriosis and infertility.

Mentally, it has been a tough journey. It is hard to lose sleep from being in pain, and having to work an eight-hour day, smiling through it all. It gets mentally exhausting. It's also hard emotionally to deal with the infertility that has resulted, and yet I have managed to get on with life and even enjoy myself more days than not.

There are days when I hate my luck for having this, but then there are days when I think of how strong of a woman I am for dealing with endometriosis. I know someone who can't handle any level of pain at all. Compared to her, I am a superhero. Endometriosis has made me a superwoman. If I can get through this, what can't I conquer in the end? I now know that I can face anything. I never would have known that about myself had it not been for suffering with endometriosis.

Another positive aspect of living with endometriosis are the relationships I have developed with others as a result of this disease. There are people in my life that I know that I can depend on, even more so because of what I've had to depend on them for while going through endometriosis. From my mom who emptied my puke bucket all those years, to my dad who has spent hours researching doctors and treatments, to my husband who has cared for me after surgery and every month when I'm moaning in pain, to the women who have supported me online and who I have supported in turn, I have realized that there are so many good, amazing people in the world. My illness has caused me to see the greatness that exists in other people, and has opened me up to trusting more and leaning on others when needed.

A final silver lining which may come to fruition is fulfilling a dream of adopting a child. When I was in elementary school, I had a conversation with my friends about how many kids we wanted to have when we were older. My answer: seven. "Seven kids?" I remember my friend Sydney saying incredulously, "That's going to hurt a lot!" We had just learned exactly how babies come out. "Well, I'm going to have one of my own. The rest I'll adopt," I responded.

In the back of my mind, that dream of adoption was something that lived on. I didn't mention it to my husband, however, until the very real possibility of not having biological children came up. We are seriously looking at adoption now, and there is a level of excitement there that persists even in the heartbreak of not being able to have a biological child. If we can't have a baby, the effort that we have gone through to try to be parents is one that we will take forward to adoption, and we will appreciate our future children even more, as my longtime dream may come true.

*

JORDANNE GOLD
Jordanne was diagnosed with
endometriosis in 2014 at age 22

My journey over the past four years has been harder mentally and physically than I could have ever imagined. Going through an illness with chronic pain changes you as a person. It gives you a new perspective on what is important in life, and shows what people will do for you, and which people won't. I lost friends and in a way I lost myself, but through that I became a new and stronger person. I gained new values and new strength, I see myself in a new light and now with a new respect. On the bad days, it is hard to respect what I had to go through. But on the good days, I am so proud of who I have become and I wouldn't want to change that for anything.

*

CHRISTA HALL
Christa was diagnosed with
endometriosis in 2015 at age 24

The silver lining that I've found with my journey is the people I've helped, and hopefully will continue to help, especially with this book. My theory on challenging and life-altering events is that there are two ways to deal with them: let them bring you down or do everything you can to turn it into a helping experience. I've always tried to help support people going through traumatic events since my brother suddenly died in 2005, so this was no different. After I was done with being angry with everything, I knew this would be no different, I wanted to help other women and make it to where it doesn't take an average of eight to ten years for a diagnosis, and to get rid of the discrimination women face with doctors about their pain.

*

BETH JENSEN
Beth was diagnosed with
endometriosis in 2009 at age 20

My silver lining is my beautiful son, who I don't think would be here today if it weren't for my fight and determination to prove doctors wrong about me, and the wonderful friends I have made along the way who regrettably share in my challenges.

*

CARMELA POLLOCK
Carmela was diagnosed with
endometriosis in 1995 at age 25

The wisdom and perspective gained from living with this disease can only be found in the struggle. The decision to have a hysterectomy catapulted me into profound and intense feelings of grief and isolation. While no medication or treatment made the endometriosis go away permanently, the removal of what I thought was the only source of my female identity compelled me to review my thinking and embrace the forgotten feminine within myself that is more than the female reproductive system—it is the mind, body, and spirit.

Acknowledging my femininity in all its aspects has been the heart of my internal happiness and most definitely the happiness I now share with my husband. I no longer suppress, neither by choice nor through conditioning, the need to fulfill societal expectations on the definition of a woman, mother or wife. It is through my life experience that I've come to understand the importance of living an authentic life, embracing all aspects of who I am and accepting those parts I have lost.

I've also come to realize that endometriosis is an experience, not just a diagnosis. It spurred challenging emotions and physical symptoms, and changed the way I think and do things. It forced me to review my life and see beauty in the struggle. I'm empowered by viewing it as an experience that presented immense personal growth and as a tangible donation to learning for all women who journey with endometriosis through authoring this book.

*

ASHLEY ROMANKO
Ashley was diagnosed with
endometriosis in 2005 at age 21

The silver lining resulting from my journey has been the women
I've met because of this disease. It's amazing to find others who just
know how it feels. They understand it all and they care. They all mean
so much to me. They are all very strong. I am so thankful to each and
every one of them. It didn't take long for me to realize this.

*

JACQUIE YOUNG
Jacquelyn was diagnosed with
endometriosis in 2012 at age 22

Although endometriosis comes with many challenges, I've found
my silver lining. Instead of looking at being sick in a negative way, I
have accepted it and have found a passion in helping others. I've
always wanted to be in the medical field, but it wasn't until this past
year when I knew I was meant to work with patients who suffer with
endometriosis. I'll use my personal experience and show my patients
empathy. So many of us just want to talk to someone who gets it. I
know that this was my path, to help others in need.

*

JENNIFER YOUNG
Jennifer was diagnosed with
endometriosis in 2009 at age 21

My silver lining is I have had to work on patience and learn to
listen to my body. I have had moments when I wanted to do something

242

and my body just would not allow whatever it was right then. I had to wait until I was doing better to do that particular activity. It took me a little bit, but I eventually figured out that if I just wait and didn't try to push too much too soon, my results would be better.

*

After all these years, I am still involved
in the process of self-discovery.
SOPHIA LOREN

*

CHAPTER EIGHTEEN

Importance of Hope

Be like the birds, sing after every storm.
-BETH MENDE CONNY

Hope is the fuel that propels us forward, urges us to get out of bed each morning. It is the promise that tomorrow will be better than today, but chronic pain has a way of redefining what hope means to each woman living with endometriosis. What does hope mean to you today?

*

ADRIEANNE BEASLEY
Adrieanne was diagnosed with
endometriosis in 2014 at age 31

Hope means that someday there will be a cure for endometriosis. I hold onto hope that one day I can live a pain-free "normal" life. Until then I will keep fighting!

*

SHILOH BRITT
Shiloh was diagnosed with
endometriosis in 2011 at age 22

Hope is believing that something good will come out of a situation, no matter how hopeless it may seem. Hope is that fleeting glimpse of a lapse of pain and the thought that there is life outside of endometriosis. In some odd way, living with endometriosis has given me hope.

*

SHANDI CLOUSE
Shandi was diagnosed with
endometriosis in 2015 at age 27

Hope to me now means the willingness to see the beauty and lessons in everything we go through, to carry on through the hardest moments we face and still be able to laugh and enjoy our lives.

Hope is continuing to battle this illness day to day and know that I'm not alone in it, that there are thousands of endometriosis sisters who feel just like I do. It's praying that a cure will be found someday, and raising awareness however I can. It's being there for someone who just got diagnosed and holding the hand of your friend who just had another surgery. Hope is the yellow bracelet I wear every day. It's in how my daughters smile when I can hoop with them, and the love in my husband's eyes on a date. It's taking it one day at a time and living my life, not just existing in it.

*

SHAUNA COX
Shauna was diagnosed with
endometriosis in 2012 at age 29

My definition of hope when it comes to endometriosis is a desire to get better and an expectation that one day I will have effective excision surgery that will "cure" me from endometriosis. I am trying as much as possible to look to the future.

When I am in the throes of a pain episode, it's hard to be hopeful. It feels like the pain is never-ending and that there is no doctor out there who could possibly help. It's hard to be hopeful when I'm so tired all the time, when the pain occurs more often than not, and when my husband and I have seemingly tried almost everything we can to get pregnant to no avail. Endometriosis has taken so much from me, and yet I know that it is not hopeless. I know that there is help out there for me, and that there is a light at the end of the endometriosis tunnel.

I found the Center for Endometriosis Care in Atlanta, Georgia and spoke to a doctor there that believes he can successfully excise the endometriosis out of me, leaving my reproductive organs and possibly increasing my fertility to the point where we may not even need assisted reproductive technologies to get pregnant! That gives me hope. Every time I'm in pain, I think to having surgery there, and to the possibility of a relief from the existence I've known for the majority of my life, and I feel a happiness and calmness come over me.

"I can get through this," I think. And, "There are doctors who can help me."

I try as much as possible to look to the good in my life. I look at the people I am lucky enough to have close to me who have supported me through everything I have been through with this disease. I look to the future, and hope for a pain-free existence not just for me, but for all the women in the world who suffer with endometriosis.

I am hopeful that there are doctors who are leading experts in their field who know how to do excision surgery. I am hopeful that books like this will come out to raise awareness and educate people on this disease. I am thrilled that there are movies coming out that are centered on endometriosis, and showing people that effective excision surgery is possible. Only through education and awareness will there be any hope in fighting this, and it looks as if things are getting better in that respect. There's hope for the future in endometriosis treatment and care, and I think it's important to focus on that as much as possible.

*

JORDANNE GOLD
Jordanne was diagnosed with
endometriosis in 2014 at age 22

Hope is knowing that no matter how bad things get, there will always be those few people who stick with you and carry you through the days you can't get through yourself.

*
CHRISTA HALL
Christa was diagnosed with
endometriosis in 2015 at age 24

Hope for me is knowing somehow, some way everything will work out the way it's supposed to, whether it's the outcome we want or not. Whether you believe in God, or the Gods and Goddesses, or just fate and destiny, we're put into situations and given challenges in life for a purpose, and one we're usually not entirely sure of. One thing I've learned that has always given me hope is knowing everything gets better, no matter how far down you are, there's always a way back up.

*
BETH JENSEN
Beth was diagnosed with
endometriosis in 2009 at age 20

Hope: That someday things will get better, just keep fighting and sharing your message, and someday you will get to live again.

*
CARMELA POLLOCK
Carmela was diagnosed with
endometriosis in 1995 at age 25

Hope wasn't something that I necessarily stored in reserve. I had to create it authentically from my lived experience and isolation with endometriosis and push forward as a promise to myself that I would see the light. I did not hope for a cure, but for a way to manage the pain and discomfort to live the best life I could.

In the weeks leading up to my hysterectomy, hope presented an opportunity to write a new chapter of my life. The bittersweet finale provided the opportunity to trust and let go of the old story to rewrite a new one. The surgery was an acknowledgment that I could release the fight, and it was okay to do so. This was part of my soul work, part of the journey. I knew this intuitively.

In moments of silence and contemplation, I had unconsciously replaced hopelessness with hope. I embraced it with an open mind and heart by acknowledging and accepting my past, and the physical pain I experienced for so many years.

Hope also revealed that my life is meant to do and not to regret. Life lessons disguised as pain, were in fact opportunities to grow. I see this now, for hope is my companion as I take the next steps in my life supporting the sacred feminine heart of other endometriosis sisters around the world.

*

ASHLEY ROMANKO
Ashley was diagnosed with
endometriosis in 2005 at age 21

My definition of hope is standing together and fighting for better treatment so that our younger generation won't have to suffer. That one day there will be a cure for endometriosis. We will no longer suffer in silence! The pain and suffering will end.

*

JACQUIE YOUNG
Jacquelyn was diagnosed with
endometriosis in 2012 at age 22

Hope has always been a word that has had many meanings to me. The two meanings that come to mind are "Hold On Pain Ends," and also to keep looking forward. We all have so much that we deal with, but if you can hold on to the idea of H.O.P.E. (Hold On Pain Ends), you will come out stronger than ever.

I always try to look ahead, even on my most challenging days. The days when I'm scared, the days when I'm so sick I can't keep water down and the pain brings me to my knees. I know I've been in those scary situations, and by looking ahead and having hope I'm able to remind myself that I've endured it before.

*

JENNIFER YOUNG
Jennifer was diagnosed with
endometriosis in 2009 at age 21

My definition of hope is trusting and believing that things will get better.

*

The sky takes on shades of orange during sunrise
and sunset, the color that gives you hope
that the sun will set only to rise again.
RAM CHARAN

*

CHAPTER NINETEEN

Finding Peace in our Journey

I don't want my pain and struggle to make me a victim. I want my battle to make me someone else's hero. -ENDOBODY

Every journey is as unique as one's fingerprint, and yet we are never truly alone, for more walk behind, beside, and in front of us. In this chapter lies the answers to the final question posed to the writers: What would you like the world to know about your journey with endometriosis?

*

ADRIEANNE BEASLEY
Adrieanne was diagnosed with
endometriosis in 2014 at age 31

I would like other women who have endometriosis to know that they are not alone in their fight and struggles with their disease. There are many outlets available for support, such as local groups.

I will not let this disease consume me and I will keep fighting and be strong no matter what. This is a disease that affects millions of women worldwide. Know that you are not alone in this!

*

SHILOH BRITT
Shiloh was diagnosed with
endometriosis in 2011 at age 22

So often we hear of endometriosis success stories, stories of triumph over infertility and pain. These stories are wonderful and all, but they did more damage than good to me. Too often, the end goal of living with endometriosis to have children. I too fell into this trap of seeing the ultimate success as giving birth to my own child. These stories are not hard to find. In fact, they are much easier to find than other ones in which the term *success* has a different definition—one that's similar to my own.

No one ever wants to have a hysterectomy, and to many living in a world with endometriosis, a hysterectomy is the ultimate form of giving up. For the longest time, I saw this procedure in the same light. When I made the decision to have my own hysterectomy at the young age of twenty-seven, I was conflicted as to whether I was giving up or not. Here's the thing I have learned in enduring all of this: having a hysterectomy is in no way giving up. It is not putting yourself before your family, spouse, or any future potential children. Having a hysterectomy is a personal decision that you and you alone can make. Having a hysterectomy is an option when all other options have failed.

Hi. My Name is Shiloh Britt, and I had a hysterectomy when I was twenty-seven years old. And you know what? Having a hysterectomy gave me back my life. True, it's an experience that I would never wish upon anyone—it's costly and affects every aspect of your physical and emotional self. It was, without a doubt, the hardest decision I've ever had to make in my young life. But was it worth it? Absolutely.

I will always have endometriosis, but having undergone a hysterectomy, I no longer feel the pain associated with it. I feel as I did before endometriosis became my life. I am free.

So what has living with endometriosis and ultimately having a hysterectomy taught me? It's simple really: It gets better.

*

SHANDI CLOUSE
Shandi was diagnosed with
endometriosis in 2015 at age 27

Even though endometriosis has been one of the most gut-wrenching parts of my life, it has taught me so much and brought some of the most beautiful people into my world. Having a chronic illness, especially at a young age, is a lot of trial and error, and living in pain changes you as a person in ways you can never understand until you personally go through it. I still have my bad days when I want to cry and scream and mourn the person I used to be, but I've learned that even those moments can be healing if I allow them to be. If nothing else, I hope that through my adversity that I can at least show my daughters that they can get through anything they may experience, as is my hope for anyone who picks this book up. Know that you are not by yourself in your journey, there are millions of us who share it with you and are here for you. Trust your instincts and never stop searching for the help you deserve. Accept the bad days with the good and put your self-care first. In the end, if my story can help even just one person know they are not alone, then it is worth every second of the pain I've gone through.

*

SHAUNA COX
Shauna was diagnosed with
endometriosis in 2012 at age 29

I have often heard people claim that if men suffered from endometriosis, there would have been a cure long ago. There wouldn't be the misconceptions there are around this disease. Doctors wouldn't be offering castration as the only option. There would be millions donated to furthering education in excision surgery. I don't know if that is true, but I do know that more needs to be done. Students in medical school need to be taught about excision surgery. They need to be given the opportunity to specialize in endometriosis because proper excision surgery is an incredibly difficult surgery to master, and not just anyone should be performing it. Doctors need to know that hormonal medications are not treatments, and that surgery is important early on to stop the disease in its tracks and to eradicate it in any woman. Women need to be better informed so that they can be their own advocates until the medical community fully catches up to the latest research.

No matter where a person is in their journey, this is a tough disease to live with. Even for people who have had excision surgery and have no more symptoms of this disease, and perhaps were lucky enough to conceive, I don't think you are ever truly rid of endometriosis. It changes a person. It changes you physically and emotionally and even if you are healed, those memories of hardship stay with you forever. I know that for me, at least, it has turned me into a fighter for others fighting a similar battle. I will fight for the teenagers who are told that they are too young to have endometriosis and are turned down from surgeries and treatments they so desperately need. I will fight for the young women who are told they need to have hysterectomies when it is not a cure for endometriosis. I will educate others at every opportunity so that people know this is not just in a person's head, and that we aren't weak or fakers or pill seekers. I want people to know that having endometriosis is hard, but that if we work together we can overcome it through educating people on the need for excision surgery and the need to take us seriously!

*

JORDANNE GOLD
Jordanne was diagnosed with
endometriosis in 2014 at age 22

My journey with endometriosis was harder than anything I could have ever imagined. It pushed me to be who I needed to be. I now spend my days working for the Alberta Endometriosis Group trying to raise awareness in society and the medical community about endometriosis. Through my journey, I learned that the world doesn't recognize or give the respect needed for women's issues. This ignorance is making a lot of women suffer, to live in pain without hope, battling mental illnesses while pressured to be quiet about it.

I want the world to know that this matters, that endometriosis is affecting millions of lives and is detrimental to our society. We deserve better than that, it is our obligation to start talking about this condition to show that our lives matter and most importantly our pain is real.

*

CHRISTA HALL
Christa was diagnosed with
endometriosis in 2015 at age 24

Living with endometriosis is difficult at best, but it doesn't mean that my world has stopped because I have a chronic pain disease. If you think that you have endometriosis, find a doctor who will listen to you, and not just brush off your symptoms or tell you that pain is just what you're supposed to deal with as a woman. As Susan Sarandon said, "It is not a woman's lot in life to suffer pain." You know your body better than any doctor can. Always keep an open line of communication with your family and friends, and never push yourself too far. Your health is your biggest priority now. If you know someone with endometriosis, support is the biggest thing they will need. This is a scary and life altering disease, but never let it define who you are.

*

BETH JENSEN
Beth was diagnosed with
endometriosis in 2009 at age 20

It's been a pretty crazy rollercoaster, but I am not my disease. I am so much more than that. Please don't just judge me by the cane I walk with, or the way I look on the outside. I've been through hell and back but I still have so much love and joy to spread to those around me.

*

CARMELA POLLOCK
Carmela was diagnosed with
endometriosis in 1995 at age 25

Working in my alternative therapies practice, I am privileged to meet women who, despite their fortitude to push through the difficult periods in their lives, including some with endometriosis, need words of encouragement and support to realize the brilliance of their body and soul in spite of the struggle they face.

The following are my final thoughts for the warrior women living with endometriosis and reading this book—in honor and love of the divine feminine that is you.

I know you are having a tough time right now, but you can do this…

You won't feel great physically or emotionally. You wish your body would just let up and be normal. I want you to know that I hear you, and all the contributors to this book hear you. You are not alone. As much as I would like to take away your pain, sadly I can't. But I can remind you that life won't always be this way. Our body changes and so do the cycles. Yes, it's tough right now, but you are tougher. You are more than the endometriosis. I know it can be hard to remember that, but can you remember all the times in your life that weren't about endometriosis? You are resilient and capable. I believe in you.

You don't have to suffer endometriosis alone...

Do you need to get in touch with a doctor, find a support group, talk to family and friends? How about practicing some self-care that lightens your heart? Being a woman can be exhausting and painful, but that's why you are a woman. You can do this, but you don't have to do it alone. The internet can be your connection to women who are struggling and suffering right along with you. Google for connections or search on Facebook. Those women are out there and waiting to hear your story and to share theirs.

Don't neglect your mental health...

Endometriosis has a way of gripping us with abdominal pain but also mental anguish. It's okay to say that you're not okay, and seek help. Please don't let stigma control your mental well-being. Let your loved ones or friends know what you are going through so they can support you. I have learned that mental illness requires a team, so if you need down time, they can be there to pick up the slack, so you don't sweat the small stuff.

Never resent your body, honor it...

It has carried you through years of pain and struggle and yet you remain standing. Honor the vessel that is you. Nurture and embrace the lessons, as unpleasant and painful as they are. The body that carries your soul makes up a brilliant system of miracles. The sum of those miracles is you. Don't let your head tell you how to feel. Don't let endometriosis magnify the negative stuff. Have the conversation with your heart. That will bring peace and gently show you the wonder that is your body.

Build your spiritual strength to lift yourself higher than your pain...

Trying to make sense of why chronic pain plagues your life will only make you crazy. Honor your moments of grace as they sculpt who you are. Listen to your divine guidance. It is always there—feel it, breathe it. Don't let the negativity muffle it because you feel pain and discomfort. Yes, life does take us off road. Living with endometriosis is full of potholes and detours. Rest assured, you will always land where you need to be.

But most of all, live with gratitude in your heart. It is a powerful healer, subtle but effective. Be it and you will see that you are your greatest gift dancing the lessons of life.

*

ASHLEY ROMANKO
Ashley was diagnosed with
endometriosis in 2005 at age 21

My journey with endometriosis is a hard one. It's a daily battle and it's one of the hardest things I've ever gone through. There's no end to the pain. Every day is a struggle. I look fine on the outside but there's so much pain on the inside. If you have endometriosis, I encourage you to get to know someone else who is going through what you are going through. Join the online support groups. Find something, no matter how small it is, to keep your mind happy and busy. Take care of yourself as best you can.

There's so much misinformation about endometriosis, and one of the things that really bothers me is the definition that doctors and nurses are learning in their textbooks, the definition that pops up when it's being googled. This definition is outdated and there is newer research to back this up. The correct definition can be found on the www.endopaedia.info website which is written by an endometriosis specialist, Dr. David Redwine. The definition from the website: Endometriosis is when tissue that somewhat resembles the lining of the womb (endometrium) is found outside the womb.

Endometriosis and endometrium are not identical; in fact there are many differences between them. Endometriosis comes in many shapes and forms and has common patterns of occurrence within the pelvis. Endometriosis can occasionally occur in other parts of the body such as in the bellybutton, lung, and brain. It has been found to occur in animals and humans, including babies, men, and postmenopausal women. It's an equal opportunity disease! The main symptom of endometriosis is chronic pelvic pain and pain during certain activities, and represents one of the most common human diseases on the face of the earth.

It's hard to explain to someone who doesn't understand how awful it is. Before my symptoms started, I wouldn't have been able to really understand either. A couple of years ago, I found the spoon theory by Christine Miserandino. It helps explain living with a chronic illness. We are given twelve spoons a day and each activity costs one spoon, such as getting out of bed, showering, breakfast, etc. By lunchtime, you have about half of the spoons you started the day with. Then you make lunch, do the dishes, maybe some other light housework, and then before dinner you have one or two spoons left. Make dinner, clean up a bit because by then you are out of spoons and therefore out of strength. You can borrow spoons from the next day, but then you have to start with less spoons tomorrow. I find that on my worst days, a shower can take five spoons instead of three. Every day is different and some days are good and some are so bad that I'm surprised I got through the day.

On the toughest days, you need to just get through the day. I just keep thinking tomorrow will be better. It's really extreme pain today and most of the day I've thought, "I can't do this...the pain is too much"

Most people can't comprehend how much pain and discomfort I have on a daily basis. I've met some amazing women who also have endometriosis. They understand everything. It's heartbreaking to know there are others dealing with this, but it's uplifting to know someone actually understands.

Everybody is different and what works for one may not work for another. I encourage you to find something that will help you get through the day. Don't give up! Don't lose hope! I will continue to fight! I will fight for my daughter! I will fight for you! I will fight so that others won't suffer as I have. We all need to support each other. We are all important. We are all in this battle together.

If you know someone with endometriosis, SUPPORT THEM. You may not even know they have the disease, they may be good at hiding it, they may not realize they even have it. You can help them. You can break the silence.

*

JACQUIE YOUNG
Jacquelyn was diagnosed with
endometriosis in 2012 at age 22

I want the world to know that my battle with endometriosis has been one of my toughest yet. From early on with my initial symptoms, I wasn't sure what was wrong with me. I went to so many doctors who didn't know how to help me, didn't know what was wrong, and some doubted that I was even sick. I want the world to know it's not okay to be in pain every day, it's not okay to miss special events because some doctor doesn't want to acknowledge that you are sick and need help. I want to educate our society about this debilitating disease. I want doctors, school nurses, teachers, parents, etc. to know the basic symptoms enough to steer her in the right direction. I will shout it from the rooftops, because this matters and so do you. You are not alone, you are not crazy. You, my friend, are in pain. Together we will win this fight.

*

JENNIFER YOUNG
Jennifer was diagnosed with
endometriosis in 2009 at age 21

That it has not been easy, it has had its up and downs. Endometriosis is one of those things that is very unpredictable......just don't get discouraged when you start off having a good day and it turns bad at the drop of a hat, because that will happen sometimes and sometimes you will start a day good and end it good. One final thought is to make friends with endometriosis sisters. When you feel like no one understands what you are going through, your endometriosis sister will.

*

She who heals others heals herself.
LYNDA CHELDELIN FELL

*

CHAPTER TWENTY

Meet the writers

*

ADRIEANNE BEASLEY
Adrieanne was diagnosed with
endometriosis in 2014 at age 31
faceitmakeupbyadrieanne.com | adrieanneb@hotmail.com

Adrieanne Beasley was born and raised in Niagara Falls, Ontario. She graduated from Niagara College as a dental assistant in 2001, and from Canadian Beauty College as certified makeup artist in 2012. She is a full-time dental assistant and owns a freelance makeup company Face It Makeup By Adrieanne.

Adrieanne enjoys spending time with her husband and friends, spending time outdoors, camping, traveling and cooking. She is also passionate about fitness and enjoys yoga, weight lifting and pole fitness. She and her husband Matt live in Edmonton, Alberta.

*
SHILOH BRITT
Shiloh was diagnosed with
endometriosis in 2011 at age 22

Shiloh Britt was born and raised in Bellingham, Washington. After high school, Shiloh studied marine science at University of Hawaii in Hilo until health concerns brought her home in 2011. Falling short of her degree, Shiloh followed her passion for caring for others and became a certified care-giver specializing in young adults with special needs. In spring 2011, Shiloh met her husband Mitch, and they married on August 16, 2014. During this time, Shiloh spent a great amount of time soul searching and came to the realization that she was happiest when outdoors. True to her

father's prediction, Shiloh resumed studies at Western Washington University in the winter of 2013, and completed her Bachelor's degree in Environmental Studies in 2016, with a minor in environmental policy and communication studies. Shiloh lives with her husband and three "kids" (cats) in Bellingham, Washington.

*

EMMA CLIFTON
Emma was diagnosed with
endometriosis in 2015 at age 30

Emma Clifton was born and raised on the Mornington Peninsula near Melbourne, Australia. She completed schooling in 2002, and started working full-time straight out of school. She was determined not to let schooling get in the way of a good career, and had always dreamed of being successful and not relying on her knight in shining armor to be the breadwinner. Emma was promoted into sales at age twenty and has been in sales and marketing ever since. Although she spent time working with big corporate companies, something was always amiss, and it was only after going through serious life battles that Emma realized what she was missing all along: passion.

After ending a very challenging long-term relationship, her father passing away, and being diagnosed with endometriosis all within a span of two years, Emma found herself at rock bottom. But something inside didn't allow her to sit in muck, so she turned to yoga and energy healing. Six months later Emma became a qualified healer and also completed training to be a yoga teacher, which changed her life.

*

SHANDI CLOUSE
Shandi was diagnosed with
endometriosis in 2015 at age 27

Shandi Clouse lives in her hometown of Tulsa, Oklahoma, with her husband Eric, her two young daughters, Trinity and Luna, and her service dog, Hades. Shandi is an accomplished alternative and tattoo model and published author, writing for websites such as Infinite Circles and A Submissive's Initiative. She also helps to run Hoopus: WereWolf HopeCraft, an organization that encourages people with chronic and mental illnesses to use hula hooping as a positive outlet. Shandi enjoys reading, painting, watching anime with her husband, and teaching her daughters to hula hoop.

*

PATRICIA CONNELLY
Patricia was diagnosed with
endometriosis in 2014 at age 33

Patricia is an amazing person who has tons of endometriosis sisters and a few friends outside of endometriosis. She lives on a small farm with her family in Oklahoma, very close to a lake. Tricia always has a smile and a hug for people she cares about.

*

SHAUNA COX
Shauna was diagnosed with
endometriosis in 2012 at age 29

Shauna Cox was born in Montreal and moved to Toronto at age thirteen. Shortly after graduating with a Specialized Honours B.A. in Psychology and a postgraduate certificate in Autism & Behavioral Sciences, she met her husband, Roger, and together they moved to St. Paul, Alberta.

Shauna works as a receptionist for a veterinary clinic, which is perfect for her love of animals. She also dreams of writing and publishing a novel one day. Shauna and Roger dream of having children, but in the meantime

they put all their attention into their three fur-babies: Riley and Roxey (two Jack Russell Terriers), and PussyBear (their cat). Shauna enjoys camping, hiking, traveling, reading and writing.

*

JORDANNE GOLD
Jordanne was diagnosed with
endometriosis in 2014 at age 22

Jordanne Gold grew up in the small town of Maple Creek, Saskatchewan. As a competitive figure skater, she learned the value of hard work, determination, and perseverance. Jordanne's skating background led her to operate her own coaching business for skating and personal training. The business continued to grow until Jordanne attended Mount Royal University to earn a Bachelor degree in Business Administration with a minor in Kinesiology. Jordanne explored different job opportunities including working as a zipline guide and doing economic development for Southeast Alberta. She loves to explore the world through traveling, hiking, and rock climbing.

*

CHRISTA HALL
Christa was diagnosed with
endometriosis in 2015 at age 24

Christa Hall was born near Cincinnati, and raised near Virginia Beach. She is self-employed and struggled for years with chronic pain. Christa finally received a diagnosis of endometriosis in December 2015, and has turned her life's mission into helping women and future generations of girls get a correct diagnosis and the support they need. Christa enjoys reading, baking and spending time with her family and closest friends.

*

BETH JENSEN
Beth was diagnosed with
endometriosis in 2009 at age 20

Beth Jensen was born in Vancouver, Canada, and moved to Edmonton at age eight. At age ten, her parents divorced and Beth began living under the sole care of her mother. She left home at seventeen and moved in with her future husband of ten years. Working full-time and living with her husband in a loving relationship, Beth graduated high school on time through distance learning. She decided to choose administrative work and soon found her niche, never forgetting her dream of becoming an accountant.

When Beth was twenty-three, she got the best surprise of her life and found out she and her husband were expecting! Later that year and after a bumpy pregnancy, Beth successfully gave birth to a healthy and beautiful baby boy. Almost a year later, in 2013, Beth married her wonderful, caring, and patient husband. In 2014, they moved to Valleyview, Alberta, moving into their new house in a quiet town closer to family. Beth is fighting against endometriosis every day, but is happy with the family she and her husband have built.

*

JESSICA NOEL
Jessica was diagnosed with
endometriosis in 1991 at age 9

Jessica Noel was born and raised in Massachusetts in both the country and city. At age nine she was diagnosed with severe, stage four endometriosis. She is now thirty-five, and still battling with it each day.

*

CARMELA POLLOCK
Carmela was diagnosed with
endometriosis in 1995 at age 25
www.soulworksessential.com

Born in Melbourne, Australia, Carmela graduated from Melbourne University with a degree in Social Sciences. She is a wife and mother of one. She has worked in information technology for over twenty years as a consultant specializing in project and change management. A voracious reader, author, and mental health advocate, Carmela actively supports a number of organizations and institutions and provides support to mental health caregivers through her voluntary work with BeyondBlue (www.beyondblue.com.au) and Deakin University, as an expert panel member to establish guidelines for carers. She founded an online community to support mental health carers in Australia and across the globe called A Black Dog About the House. Carmela co-authored *Grief Diaries: Grieving for the Living,* where she shares her story of supporting a partner with depression. Carmela has retrained, turning her focus to health and well-being. She is the director, certified counsellor and Usui Reiki Master Teacher of Soulworks Essential Therapies. Her goal is to guide individuals to embrace discovering health and wellness from within using alternative therapies to complement Western medicine.

*

ASHLEY ROMANKO
Ashley was diagnosed with
endometriosis in 2005 at age 21
Alberta Endometriosis Facebook Support Group
Facebook.com/groups/1484024298527300
ashleyrendomarch.alberta@gmail.com

Ashley Romanko was born and raised in Edmonton, Canada. She is the founder of the Facebook group Alberta Endometriosis Group. She is a wife and mother of two children, a nine-year-old daughter, Alexandra, and five-year-old son William. She has a three-year-old dog named, Buddy. Ashley has an amazing, supportive husband, Darren. Some of her hobbies include scrapbooking, coloring, vintage finds, walking, baking, cooking, beadwork, reading, crocheting and sewing. She hasn't been able to work in years because of severe endometrial pain.

*

SAYDA WYMER
Sayda was diagnosed with
endometriosis in 2010 at age 35

Sayda Wymer was born in Nicaragua and moved to the United States at age eleven. She grew up in Fort Worth, Texas, and joined the U.S. Navy in 1998. She married her husband Jack and has two healthy boys, Joseph and Jaden. She completed her military tour in 2002, and became a stay-at-home mom. She then completed pharmacy technician school and became a licensed pharmacy technician. She is hard working, devoted and dedicated to her family. She loves to spend time with her husband and kids, and treasures every moment with her children.

*

JACQUIE YOUNG
Jacquelyn was diagnosed with
endometriosis in 2012 at age 22

Jacquie Young was raised outside of Pittsburgh, Pennsylvania. She is a professional makeup artist and plans to finish her nursing degree. She currently lives in Boston with her husband, Josh.

*

JENNIFER YOUNG
Jennifer was diagnosed with
endometriosis in 2009 at age 21

Jennifer Young was born in South Bend, Indiana. She married the love of her life, Keith, and they live in De Queen, Arkansas. She and Keith have two little miracles, four-year-old Adalina and two-year-old Gaige. They also live with the family dogs Gunner, a German Shepherd mix, Winter, a Catahoula and Australian Shepherd mix, and Gypsie, a Blue Tick-Pitt Bull mix. Jennifer is a stay-at-home mom who would like to eventually return to school. She hopes her story will give hope to all who read it.

THANK YOU

I am deeply indebted to the writers who contributed to Real Life Diaries: Living with Endometriosis. It requires tremendous courage to pen intimate details of our lives for the purpose of helping others, and the collective dedication to seeing this project through is a legacy the writers can be proud of. I'm humbled to partner with coauthors Christa Hall and Carmela Pollock, two ladies I admire immensely for their advocacy work and planting seeds of hope.

It's been said that pictures alone, without the written word, leaves half the story untold. A good story intrigues and invites us to go beyond the edge of our own life into the world of another where we discover, learn, find commonalities and—perhaps most important— we leave with deeper understanding of one another. That's what Real Life Diaries is all about.

Lynda Cheldelin Fell

One smile can change a mood.
One hello can change a day.
One story can change a life.
LYNDA CHELDELIN FELL

*

ABOUT

LYNDA CHELDELIN FELL

Considered a pioneer in the field of inspirational hope, Lynda Cheldelin Fell has a passion for producing projects that create a legacy of help, healing, and hope.

She is an international best-selling author and creator of the award-winning book series Grief Diaries and Real Life Diaries. She earned four national literary awards in 2016, and nominated for five national health advocacy awards in 2017. Her repertoire of interviews include Dr. Martin Luther King's daughter, Trayvon Martin's mother, sisters of the late Nicole Brown Simpson, Pastor Todd Burpo of Heaven Is For Real, and other societal newsmakers on finding healing and hope in the face of harsh challenges.

Lynda's own story began in 2007, when she had an alarming dream about her young teenage daughter, Aly. In the dream, Aly was a backseat passenger in a car that veered off the road and landed in a lake. Aly sank with the car, leaving behind an open book floating face down on the water. Two years later, Lynda's dream became reality when her daughter was killed as a backseat passenger in a car accident while coming home from a swim meet. Overcome with grief, Lynda's forty-six-year-old husband suffered a major stroke that left him with severe disabilities, changing the family dynamics once again.

The following year, Lynda was invited to share her remarkable story about finding hope after loss, and she accepted. That cathartic experience inspired her to create groundbreaking projects spanning national events, radio, film and books to help others who share the same journey feel less alone. Now a passionate curator of stories, Lynda is dedicated to helping people share their own extraordinary journeys that touch the hearts of readers around the world.

lynda@lyndafell.com | www.lyndafell.com

ALYBLUE MEDIA TITLES

Real Life Diaries: Living with Endometriosis
Real Life Diaries: Living with Mental Illness
Real Life Diaries: Living with Rheumatic Disease
Real Life Diaries: Living with a Brain Injury
Real Life Diaries: Through the Eyes of DID
Real Life Diaries: Through the Eyes of an Eating Disorder
Real Life Diaries: Living with Gastroparesis
Real Life Diaries: Through the Eyes of a Funeral Director
Grief Diaries: Surviving Loss of a Spouse
Grief Diaries: Surviving Loss of a Child
Grief Diaries: Surviving Loss of a Sibling
Grief Diaries: Surviving Loss of a Parent
Grief Diaries: Surviving Loss of an Infant
Grief Diaries: Surviving Loss of a Loved One
Grief Diaries: Surviving Loss by Suicide
Grief Diaries: Surviving Loss of Health
Grief Diaries: How to Help the Newly Bereaved
Grief Diaries: Loss by Impaired Driving
Grief Diaries: Loss by Homicide
Grief Diaries: Loss of a Pregnancy
Grief Diaries: Hello from Heaven
Grief Diaries: Grieving for the Living
Grief Diaries: Shattered
Grief Diaries: Project Cold Case
Grief Diaries: Poetry & Prose and More
Grief Diaries: Through the Eyes of Men
Grief Diaries: Will We Survive?
Grief Diaries: Hit by Impaired Driver
Grammy Visits From Heaven
Grandpa Visits From Heaven
Faith, Grief & Pass the Chocolate Pudding
Heaven Talks to Children
God's Gift of Love: After Death Communication
Color My Soul Whole
Grief Reiki

Humanity's legacy of stories and storytelling
is the most precious we have.

DORIS LESSING

*

To share your story, visit
www.griefdiaries.com

PUBLISHED BY ALYBLUE MEDIA
Inside every human is a story worth sharing.
www.AlyBlueMedia.com

Printed in Great
Britain
by Amazon

31608275R00180